WHO WAS JESUS OF NAZARETH? AND OTHER STUDIES

Published @ 2017 Trieste Publishing Pty Ltd

ISBN 9780649733538

Who Was Jesus of Nazareth? And Other Studies by James Alex. Robertson

Edited by Trieste Publishing Pty Ltd.
Cover @ 2017

www.triestepublishing.com

JAMES ALEX. ROBERTSON

WHO WAS JESUS OF NAZARETH? AND OTHER STUDIES

Trieste

WHO WAS JESUS OF NAZARETH?

BY THE SAME AUTHOR

THE SPIRITUAL PILGRIMAGE OF JESUS.
Fifth Impression. 6s. net.

THE HIDDEN ROMANCE OF THE NEW
TESTAMENT. Fourth Impression. 6s. net.

DIVINE VOCATION IN HUMAN LIFE.
6s. net.

CONCERNING THE SOUL. 6s. net.

JESUS THE CITIZEN. 5s. net.

JAMES CLARKE & CO., LIMITED
9, ESSEX STREET, LONDON, W.C.2

WHO WAS
JESUS OF NAZARETH?

AND OTHER STUDIES

BY

JAMES ALEX. ROBERTSON, M.A., D.D.

PROFESSOR OF NEW TESTAMENT LANGUAGE, LITERATURE
AND THEOLOGY, UNITED FREE CHURCH COLLEGE, ABERDEEN;
AUTHOR OF "THE SPIRITUAL PILGRIMAGE OF JESUS," "THE
HIDDEN ROMANCE OF THE NEW TESTAMENT," "JESUS THE
CITIZEN," ETC., ETC.

LONDON
JAMES CLARKE & COMPANY, LIMITED
9, ESSEX STREET, STRAND, W.C.2

Printed in Great Britain

Preface

THIS book consists of Lectures and Papers gathered together from various directions. The first chapter, entitled: " Who was Jesus of Nazareth ? " was a Murtle Lecture, delivered in Aberdeen University. The second, " The Master Teacher," was an address given at a convention of the Scottish National Sabbath School Union held in Dundee. The next two—on the Atonement—appeared in *The Expository Times*. The sixth, on " The Mind of the Master on Immortality," was prepared as an inaugural lecture for one winter's course of the Aberdeen School of Study and Training for Christian Workers. The seventh, on "The Authority of Scripture," was a paper read before the Christian Unity Association of Scotland. And the last was the inaugural lecture delivered on assuming the duties of the Chair of New Testament Language and Literature in the Aberdeen United Free Church College. Though thus widely separate in purpose and occasion, they embody thoughts on some leading topics of New Testament Theology, and may be found to have a certain unity of outlook. They are here collected in this more permanent form, at the request of friends, in the hope that they may be of some service.

Contents

I

Who was Jesus of Nazareth?

I

WHEN President Woodrow Wilson published his
fourteen epoch-making points, which released a
fettered world from the iron prison-house of war, a
London journalist, who could not be accused of
religious bias, said they were read by more people
than were the words of any other man since Jesus of
Nazareth. How was it that almost unconsciously
this man gave Jesus of Nazareth the highest place?
How has it come to be universally admitted that the
words of Jesus are the words which have had the
profoundest significance in the history of mankind?
What is the meaning of the fact that the world's
greatest possession consists of two or three hundred
sayings uttered in a tiny strip of country situated
between the desert and the sea?

Was it the accident of a good platform? The
Land of Palestine, but for its religious story, is
insignificant. True, it was sometimes called " The
Bridge," for the long stony ridge of it, separated
from the desert by a deep river gorge, and fronting
the Mediterranean with an almost harbourless coast-
line, was none the less the link between the ancient

9

civilisations of Egypt and Assyria, and still to-day may almost be said to be the meeting-ground of three continents. Yet that would be nothing if the words spoken there had been empty or unworthy. The separateness of land and people made the region the natural home of oblivion, to whose hungry devouring maw mere words are an easy prey. The cry of the wild bird in a lonely place is soon swallowed up in the everlasting taciturnity, because the wild bird's cry is monotonous and mindless repetition. The very environment testifies therefore to the fact that the utterer of these supreme words was no echo but a voice. He did not even write the words. So far as we know His only writing was with His finger in the dust of the Temple flagstones in Jerusalem. The next gust of wind swirled these hieroglyphics all away. His words depend for their immortality in the first instance on frail mortal memories, the memories of those who heard. Yet they live on, and perennially revitalise the spirit of man. To-day they are being listened to in all quarters of human society—even in the most unlikely—as are no other words in any language or of any age. Who was their utterer ?

And immediately from one direction comes the retort, "What does it matter ? The message of the words themselves is everything, the man who spoke them nothing." We would be the last to deny the greatness of the message. The sublimest philosopher has never set before the world an ideal for humanity

that outreaches it. Jesus spoke of a spiritual Kingdom, a kingdom of Humanity, a Kingdom of God.
And the principles of that Kingdom—described in
words that have wings of fire and hands that grip the
heart and will not let it go—are recognised far and
wide to-day as containing in essence the solution alike
of the social problem and of the international tangle.
A new mood, a new attitude has come into the mind
of man with regard to them in recent years. It was
the fashion of yesterday to consider them dreamy
and impracticable. To-day they are voted intensely
real and practical—the only genuine *Real-politik* that
exists. The Covenant of the League of Nations,
which is steadily winning recognition as the only
hope of the salvation of the world from war, is,
whatever be its imperfections, the greatest concrete
embodiment of the ideal of Jesus since He Himself
walked the fields and streets of Palestine. It is
impossible for us to-day to ignore the marvel of the
message. But it is that very wonder which compels
us to ask about the Man who uttered it.

Can we separate the Man from His Message ?
Is it a purely academic question ? Do we settle the
question by asking with a smile, Who wrote the plays
of Shakespeare ? Shakespeare or Bacon ? Consider
it a moment. Prove—if you can—that Bacon wrote
these plays. Do you discredit the plays thereby ?
You only compel us to revise fundamentally our
judgment of Bacon. Who wrote the Iliad or the
Odyssey ? A vast amount of energy and ink has been

spilt over the problem. Do you abolish Homer by proving it was another person of the same name ? Either way, the poems demonstrate the existence of a great poet. It was early debated whether the dialogue " Phaedo " was written by Plato. Surely the epigram is not only witty but full of sound commonsense : εἰ με Πλάτων οὐ γράψε, δυο ἐγένοντο Πλάτωνες. (If Plato did not write me, there were two Platos). May we not claim it as equally true that the great words from Palestine proclaim the greatness of their Author ?

It is not *our* age that has invested the words with a splendour and power that is alien to them. It is not a mere accident of *our* day that they have leapt into life and become operative. They have been at work in the world for nigh two thousand years. The course of the centuries is starred with the *Gesta Christi*. Again and again blots in pagan, mediæval and modern life—infanticide, the amphitheatre, slavery—have been cleansed out by their influence. As the ages pass it grows clearer and clearer that they are the charter of the rights and duties of man. Europe is strewn with great cathedral piles built in the name of Him who spoke these words. Look back from some eminence on the spires of this city of ours. Who built them ? Multiply it by every city in the land, and add the churches in every country dale and plain. " Emerson," said Carlyle to his friend as they looked down on the Kirk of Dunscore, " Jesus Christ was crucified eighteen hundred years ago. Jesus Christ built that kirk. Jesus Christ brought you and me together here." " In the heart of the remotest mountains," the same prophet once wrote, " rises the little kirk, speaking things unspeakable, and changing for many a soul this vague, shoreless universe into a firm city and dwelling which he knows." To think only in this concrete way for a moment, all this mass of noble masonry is the confession of the world's glorious failure to separate the Man from His Message.

But yet another voice of colossal effrontery stops us here, and says, All these vast cathedrals and innumerable churches are built upon a lie. There never was any Jesus. There never was any single mind behind the great words. They just filtered into, or coalesced and crystallised in, the group mind of an obscure religious sect, out of the thought atmosphere of the time. There is hardly a trace of such a man in contemporary secular history. Surely that is a perverse obsession. Because those traces of His activity are so faint and meagre, is that any reason for explaining the apparently offending sentences in Tacitus, Suetonius and Pliny away ? We would rather pin our faith to that ounce of historic testimony than to the tons of theory that have been heaped up about Jesus' non-existence. But the significance of men and movements is not to be estimated by the evidence of contemporary historians. It is the subsequent course of history that is the true demonstration of the value of historic fact. Is the universe so built that it makes use of delusion, deception and fraud to further the highest ends of life ? Is not the history of the world the judgment of the world ? Or must we fling it all aside at the dictation of some wayward minds ?

II

Who then was Jesus ? Why does this question keep repeating itself ? Is it because the records are so dim and hazy and uncertain, and we want to be sure of the truth of them ? Yes, but *why* do we want to know ? The very fact that we ask this question is itself a kind of answer. Concerning no other founder of a religion does such a question ever become strident. And so far as the mere external aspect of this man's life is concerned, there is no great difficulty about the facts. A village Carpenter, brought up in poverty and obscurity, toiled till the age of thirty at the bench, began to speak to the crowds in the Highlands of Galilee, healed the sick, by and by came into collision with the ecclesiastical authorities of the day, and at the end of perhaps three years' propaganda, suffered the extreme penalty at the hands of the Roman Procurator, Pontius Pilate. We have no sooner set that down than up comes the question again, Yes, but who was He ?

And at last the true nature of the question begins to grow clear. It is not mere historic certainty or information we are seeking. It is a judgment as to this Man's significance in the life of mankind. It is what the philosopher calls a value-judgment we are after. And it is not merely What do His thoughts signify for us ? But, What does He Himself, His personality, signify for us ? And since personality is the meeting-point of history and religion, this does not cease to be a historical question when it becomes a religious question.

Let us go back to where the question first emerges in Christian thought. The earliest records of the faith which we possess are some four or five letters of St. Paul. The most searching and the most sceptical enquirers have been compelled to admit their authenticity. And here we are immediately confronted with the astounding fact that an arch-Pharisee who began his career by hounding to death, in bitter and malignant hate, the followers of the crucified Carpenter, ends by being captured and enthralled by the Cross. " God forbid that I should glory," he writes in one of these letters, " save in the Cross of our Lord Jesus Christ." What does it mean ? It means that he is convinced that the Man who hung there was fulfilling by that very act the holiest purpose ever conceived in the mind of God. " Jesus is Lord." That is St. Paul's creed in brief but sufficient formula. The Jesus of history is Lord of the Universe. That is a judgment rooted and grounded in history—on as stark and grim a tragedy as ever occurred ; but it is a religious judgment, a judgment out of the depths of this Pharisee's passionate soul. How did it come about that this man should have taken that pitiful and apparently insignificant tragedy, that horrible surd in human life—rooted and grounded in history—and say that it reached out into eternity ?

The *prima facie* answer is to say it was due to the resurrection of Jesus from the dead and to Paul's own experience of it. But could the resurrection of any ordinary man have produced this result ? Assuredly not. It was only because the resurrection was congruent with all that went before. Fundamentally it must have been because of what he had learned about the man Himself—some compelling wonder about His character, His personality. Or was it that St. Paul had gone mad, and hastened through Asia and Europe raising the commotion he did, all because he was suffering from a persistent and incurable delusion ? That suggestion has sometimes been made. But the answer to it is obvious. Hundreds of persons who had followed Jesus in His lifetime were still alive when St. Paul began his propaganda. Some of them conceived a strong antipathy to this renegade Sheriff of the Sanhedrin. They followed him about and tried to thwart his efforts constantly. But did ever any of them try to controvert his judgment about the man Jesus ? Not one ! Were they all mad ? And are we to-day still at the mercy of this strange madness when we try to form our opinion about Jesus ?

Who was Jesus of Nazareth?

III

Here we are driven back to the records of His life in the Gospels. But they too, men tell us, are tainted with this madness; full of strange and incredible things, a farrago of magic and contradictions. Let us set aside for the present the so-called magic. What of the Figure that walks through these pages? How do the writers of the Gospels describe this Man, living in extreme poverty and disappearing in a great darkness at the end? What of the character, the inner soul of Jesus? Are we not, in candour, driven to this assertion about the picture there portrayed, that in the naïve, objective, unpsychological age in which it was drawn, it was utterly impossible for anyone to have invented it, and accordingly it must have been drawn from life? "It is far more incomprehensible," says Rousseau, " that many men should have agreed to compose this book than that one man alone should have provided it with its subject-matter. . . . So impossible of imitation are the characteristics of the Gospels that the man who invented them must be greater than his hero." The testimony of the Gospels convinces us that any other view than that the character of Jesus is real, authentic, and historical amounts to a *reductio ad absurdum*.

Begin to look at the picture on its most distinctively human side. One of the most striking human traits of Jesus was His capacity for fellowship. He made it His vocation to win the fellowship of the spiritually diseased and broken. Sophisticated people hardly regarded His immediate bodyguard as presentable : four fishermen, one of them a rough, blustering, swearing fellow who disgraced himself the night before the Cross ; two execrated tax-gatherers, classed by public opinion with the outcasts of society ; one pugnacious rebel whom the Romans might have hanged, carrying in his unregenerate days a dagger beneath his cloak ; one creature who sold his master at the end. Most of the so-called " better-class " people shunned Jesus, could not understand that sort of thing. Yet He could make Himself at home in any social circle. And we find Nicodemus, member of the inner circle of the supreme Jewish Council, stealing through the dark to interview Him, risking all the obloquy of his caste, risking even his life to pay this excommunicated criminal's dead body the last offices of love in sincerest veneration. We see Jesus entertained sometimes by a Pharisee. But we see the clash of the two extremes when He shocked one of them in his own house, by permitting a poor creature, down and out, the lowest of the low, weeping, to kiss His feet, and wipe the tears from them with her hair, and anoint them with precious nard. Another day a synagogue ruler kneels at this artisan-reformer's feet beseeching the help which he knew was sure to come. Even a young aristocrat, who had everything the world could bestow, comes running in his eagerness, and then kneeling, to question Him about eternal life.

Who was Jesus of Nazareth ?

Shortly after He is the guest of a little insignificant money-grubber who has been elbowed out of the crowd, having invited Himself over the heads of a sea of scowling faces. And all too soon thereafter He befriends a thief on the neighbour cross to His own, while the crowds are jeering underneath. A sorry companion with whom to pass out into the Unseen! Truly a motley throng were the many souls He befriended. But did ever any of them, high or low, make too free with Him? True they were sometimes almost riotously happy in His company. But His own dignity was never compromised. None of the disreputable associates ever presumed on His companionableness, ever slipped over the threshold of the inner sanctities. Could that picture have been invented?

Jesus was perfectly natural, simple, unassuming. He never professed to be anything but lowly. And yet—how men hung on His words, murmuring below their breath, and sometimes openly, in astonishment and awe. When He spoke, it was the last word. No one ever spoke like Him, they said. There was a strange majesty in the lowliness of this Man. His was a conscience throbbing with sincerity, challenging the ancient law which had made men stand in fear before it; a voice of solitary moral authority, making the most extraordinary demands on His followers. Simplicity and profundity, gentleness and authority, meekness and majesty, tenderness and sternness, helpfulness of love yet aloofness of purity ; apparent contradiction yet harmony, poise and power ; could any writer of the day have invented that picture ?

Courage ? The members of the Sanhedrin rubbed their eyes and stared at two bold followers after He was dead ; and they said, Oh, yes, they were companions of the Nazarene : that is how it is. Courage ? Is there any scene in history to compare with the scene in Caiaphas' judgment hall ? This spectacle of Christ confronting His enemies has been called the scene of which humanity has most reason to be proud. He was peerless in gallantry, and yet tender-hearted as a woman. Everyone felt that His compassion was far other than the comfortable pity of the bystander. He was no looker-on at wretchedness from the outside. Every poor sufferer in body, mind or conscience felt that somehow He had taken his or her place. He not merely stood beside them but identified Himself with them. " Himself *took* our infirmities, and *bore* our sicknesses." That is how, one likes to think, Levi the taxgatherer put it, quoting an ancient prophecy. It cost Him all that the sons of misery suffered and more. Courage and compassion so joined ? Had any one of that day tried to create that picture, it would have fallen to pieces in his hands. But here on the Gospel page it all blends in a perfect harmony, a character woven without seam throughout.

And His courage is but an aspect of what pervaded His whole nature, His whole life—His serenity, His imperturbable calm. It is the serenity seen in His submission to earthly parents after His discovery of God as His Father, the calm that led Him down from the communion of the mount of transfiguration to the valley of conflict and suffering, the calm of triumph surmounting the foreboding of the upper room. Outwardly regarded His life was a storm-centre ; about Him the tempests of social malice, opposition and hate gathered and fell. Yet He moves through it all with the same majestic placidity. He never was self-betrayed. His defiance of Herod's designs against Him is characteristic of His whole bearing. "Tell that fox I am going on with my work to-day, and to-morrow, and the next day I will complete it. I am going on to Jerusalem to-day, and to-morrow, and the next day ; and then and there I shall face the end." It is always the same figure that emerges in every situation ; the same radiance that shines behind the varying lights and shadows of emotion ; for He was by no means statuesque or passionless. Does He exult ? It is the pure and peaceful joy of dawn. Does He weep ? There is a quiet dignity in His tears. Is He angry ? There is towering majesty in His moral indignation. Is there a popular clamour to make Him king—political leader ? He refuses and eludes the crowd, then spends a solitary night on the hill-top, acquiring fresh calm beneath the everlasting composure of the stars. Is there agony, wrestling, bloody sweat in the garden ? Yes, but still the same steadfast submission to the dictates of His noble ideal of service ; still the same unbroken obedience to the Will of God, whom He calls that night with a child's intimate confidence, Abba, Abba. Is He in hot conflict with His enemies, or in intimate converse with His friends ? He is ever the same, always master of Himself, never caught off His guard. No sudden change in the situation— and they were often dramatic enough—ever found or made Him less than Himself. Immovable self-control ! And because of it, master always of the outward situation ; so much so that a note of ironic humour creeps sometimes into His words. Master of circumstances, captain of His soul ! "My peace," He says—and it was the peace of a man set free from the strain and struggle and striving which characterises the inner life of all other men ; the peace of a man who, spiritually, had arrived; the peace of a heart at rest—at the secret source of every precious thing. It was in part this peace, this ineffable serenity, that changed the Cross from being a meaningless thing, a stumbling block, a degradation, a curse, into something that redeems life from being a comedy of the gods into a revelation of the Father. We have no sooner spoken that word, than the question breaks out again, louder than ever, Who then was He ? What does it all imply ?

And when we proceed to cast our plummet further into the deeps of the secret we touch another amazing fact, again solitary in human history : the discord of sin never penetrated this life. Just because of its uniqueness this fact too has not gone unchallenged. We are reminded that He repudiated the epithet " Good " once. But it is sheer perversion to twist this into a confession of sin. Like Socrates, who stood before the inexhaustibility of knowledge, the overarching starry radiance of the Divine Omniscience, and said that he knew nothing, yet was conscious that he was a stage further on than other men, so with the clear, open-eyed wonder of a child this Man stood on the earth, the outer court of the Temple of cosmic holiness, and knew that He drew all His resources of good from the original Fountain of Goodness, God the alone Good. On earth He walked the moral way with other men, and this question of His—" Why callest thou Me good ? " — is but His confession that He learned obedience through suffering. His was no hedged and shaded life. All His life long He was tempted—tempted by all life's sharp contrasts. The night before He was done to death, He spoke of His whole career as " My temptations." He was tempted at the Baptism by the vision of His tremendous destiny, tempted by His mother's fond pride, tempted by His brothers' sneers, tempted by the sceptics who asked a sign, tempted by success when the people would fain have made Him king, tempted by apparent failure in His own land and by the call of the Gentile world, tempted to forego His Passion by the specious voice of prudence, speaking in an impulsive disciple. Yes, His was no cloistered virtue, no sentimental pattern of perfection ; it was one long struggle against insidious suggestion. Tempted—yet without sin. That is the subduing thing. When one watches the rain-clouds sweeping along the giant shoulders of the hidden mountains, listens to the wind roaring down the gullies, to the avalanche's tumult down the precipice, to the thunder crashing in the valleys, and later beholds the clouds roll up from off the stainless Alpine peaks, purity outreaching purity, like the first of the steps of the great white throne, one is awed by the contrast. So Christ's sinlessness against the background of His temptations overwhelms us.

To some it is unbelievable. Yet what have their searchings discovered ? Anger, harshness, contempt they point to. But rightly understood the harshness vanishes, the contempt justifies itself. And as for the anger surely there were times when the sin would have been failure to be angry. Is there anywhere any personal bitterness against His foes, any false leniency towards His friends ? Can we point to any injuring, idle word, any mistaken or wrongful zeal ? Was there ever anyone who knew the difference between right and wrong, who probed to the secret heart of sin, as He did ? Surely such a sensitive conscience could not have failed to confess His sin, if He *had* been sinful. But where is the confession ? Did ever this preacher of repentance class Himself with the sinner and say " we " ? Did He ever pray for His own forgiveness ? In the hour of the anguish of death we might expect the mask to fall. But listen : it is a prayer for others : " Father, forgive them, for they know not what they do." Listen again : " It is finished "—the verdict on His life, pronounced by Himself. It is no use to say we have only the most meagre and fragmentary record of His life ; that words of personal penitence privately spoken as they must usually be—have escaped the record. The fact remains that we have words in the record, which are simply a psychological impossibility on the lips of a sinner. He sometimes does not point beyond Himself to God, He says " Come to Me." He calls Himself the Healer of the sin-broken, He offers the Divine forgiveness, He challenges the Mosaic Law, He assumes the *rôle* of judge. And, in His presence, the conscience acknowledges His right to judge. See Him when they bring the sinful woman to Him in the Temple courts : judging by His vicarious shame-bearing— in an awesome silence. It is the judgment seat of God set up for a moment on earth. Silently, one by one, they steal away.

IV

Who was this Man ? Does not this intense, searching, judging moral chastity drive us to cast our plummet deeper still, if we can ? And the secret is there in the records, too. This flawless character flows from His abiding and unbroken sense of the presence of God in His life. The very cry of

dereliction in the hour of death testifies to it. It is
written plain and ineffaceable throughout the records.
It leaps out from His words, His movements, His
gestures even, in the most natural, and sometimes in
the most unobtrusive of ways. It cannot be gainsaid.
And it is utterly impossible for even the subtlest
psychological fictionist to have invented and carried
through so faultlessly, so inevitably, this secret of
His mind and character.

Familiar enough is that inexpressible sense of the
presence of the unseen in the lives of the great mystics
and saints. Yet at best it is but a dim adumbration
of Jesus' consciousness of God. The world-forsaking
rapture of the mystic is but star-light compared with
the deep day-clear fellowship of Jesus with Him
whom He ever called " My Father." Never even
the recollection of a yearning sigh for renewal of a
lost fellowship with God trembles in His prayer. It
was not merely from vigils of the night that He
stepped before men with the air of the presence-
chamber clinging still about Him. We recognise
the breath of the Divine Presence fanning His cheeks,
the light of it reflected in His eyes, right in the heart
of His intercourse with the waking world. From the
time when He was twelve years old at least, He called
God " My Father." It is true that when He talks
to men about God, He calls Him " your Father."
But the only recorded occasion when He said " Our
Father," was when he said, " After this manner
therefore pray *ye* "(not " pray we "). If the broken,

fragmentary records do not permit us to be sure that He never associated Himself with men in this way, nevertheless they are so consistent on the point that we can be certain this was His habit at least. Moreover the times when He says " My Father " are all, without exception, times when He is either emphasising His own special intimacy, or making some announcement about the mind of God, which He knows as the result of that intimacy. But there is hardly a word that came from His lips, that does not breathe the atmosphere of that intimacy. Once or twice without any qualification He calls Himself " the Son."

Let me refer to one saying for a moment ; because one of the most sceptical of the critics has called it one of the five foundation pillars on which we can build in recovering the picture of the historical Jesus. Speaking of the final establishment of God's Kingdom on earth, Jesus once said, " Of that day and that hour knoweth no man, not even the angels in heaven, neither the Son, save My Father only." It is a precious word to this critic because Jesus is expressly disclaiming prescience, disclaiming personal knowledge about the time of the fulfilment of God's plans. Because Jesus belittles Himself in this way, it is, to this scholar, a genuine word. Granted. But think again. What place is Jesus giving Himself ? Among men ? Nay, not in the ranks of men. On a level with angelic beings ? No ! Above all men, above even the angels in heaven, next to God

Who was Jesus of Nazareth?

Himself in the heavenly counsels. And He calls Himself " the Son " and God " My Father." It is an outstandingly significant word. With all our heart, we thank the critic for leaving us this word.

For with it many another amazing word comes stealing back proclaiming that He knew Himself to be called to a supreme *rôle*. A vocation to manifest the agonising love of God in the midst of our broken humanity in order that the union of man with God might be achieved in reconciliation. And it is here that we touch the borders of the innermost secret of the Personality of Jesus, that mysterious element of it which constitutes Him Master and Lord, which sets Him over against our lives and constrains us to worship and adore. Into the heart of it we can but dimly penetrate, and only upon our knees. "No man knoweth the Son save the Father only, and no man knoweth the Father save the Son, and he to whomsoever the Son will reveal Him." . . . " The Son of man came not to be ministered unto, but to minister, and to give His life a ransom for many."

Can we rise to the height of the demand on our credence made by these great words ? Or must our already hesitating minds here come to a dead stop ? Must we call him extravagant dreamer, madman ? How can we thereby stultify all that we have already admitted about the uninventibility of His character ? There is only one way out of the dilemma. We must admit that this consciousness of standing in a unique relation to God and to men is an undeniable part of Jesus' mind, and not only entirely congruent with, but absolutely demanded by, His character. We must confess that by His perfect response to the pressure and solicitation of the Spiritual World, that Spiritual World was finding and even now finds perfect access to the life of Humanity through Him. That in His constant dwelling in the life of God, God dwelt and evermore dwells completely in Him. That through His perfect obedience to the Will of God, God has accomplished His supreme purpose for mankind; and has come down all the way, completely to meet our struggling humanity. That because it was Christ's vocation to mediate God's forgiveness to men, His Passion was all the agony of the sin-bearing God. That because in Him finitude saw into the heart of the Unseen Godhead, in Him the Godhead has looked out on us from the seen. That because He alone has achieved the right to man's forfeited primacy in Creation, He is now to men God's eternal Speech, the Word of whom all creation is speaking in dim detail. That He has carried His manhood into the Godhead, and now as the head of the Mystical Body of believers, seeks through the Eternal Spirit to incarnate the Divine in Humanity.

In face of all that He said and did, and still does, we must bow before Him, surrendering to Him our faith. These words of mine may express it in a way you cannot wholly give your assent to, or they

Who was Jesus of Nazareth?

may be inadequate to what your faith demands. The primary essential is that our attitude to Him should be right. The test of genuine Christian faith is, Can we call Him Lord? Can we say, I believe in God through Jesus Christ, His only Son, our Lord?

The Master Teacher

TEACHER was the name by which all men called Him. It needed the Cross before men learned to call Him Saviour. Not till after Pentecost was He, in the full sense of the term, called Lord. Only once, in a supreme moment in the Galilean days, did Peter dare to name him " Christ—Messiah, Son of God." It was sometimes matter for the speculative wonder of crowds and kings, whether He was a new prophet, or one of the old prophets returned to earth. It was the constant subject of debate in the circle of His enemies, who, in the name of God, He could be. But no one, whether stranger or follower, friend or foe, ever doubted that He was the Teacher.

Yet was it not a strange name to give Him ? It was a title of honour, reserved for the scholar and the religious teacher of the day, reserved for an order with a religious sense of its vocation and power. But what were Jesus' credentials ? He had attended the synagogue school in Nazareth, no doubt, when a boy. But when school days were over, He went back to the carpenter's bench, and learned the use of hammer and saw. He had supplied the workers in Nazareth and Capernaum with " ploughs and yokes and spades." He came from the bench to teach, His hands rough with the marks of His trade. It was an offence to the people of His native town that the common artisan whom they all knew should set himself up to be a teacher. And yet they all wondered at the words of charm which came from His lips. "He speaks with an authority far beyond the Scribes," said the men of Capernaum. For they too were astonished at His teaching. When his enemies said, " Whence hath this man letters ? He never was to college," there was scorn in their tones, no doubt, but it was amazement that was uppermost. Whenever the Rabbis tried to challenge His teaching, He was more than a match for them—routed them off the field. Yes, grudgingly and reluctantly though it came from the lips of some, Master, Rabbi, Teacher He was by universal acknowledgment. "He taught" is the word used in the Gospels, far oftener than " He preached." Teacher was His disciples' favourite name for Him.

But think of the motley crowd besides, who called Him by that name. Nicodemus, chief doctor of the Law in the Temple College, was but voicing the opinion of his set when he said, " Rabbi, we know Thou art a teacher come from God." Simon the Pharisee called Him Teacher. The messengers from Jairus' house of mourning spoke of Him as the Teacher. The man with the epileptic boy beneath the Mount of Transfiguration addressed Him so. He was named Teacher by the lawyer who once stood up to tempt Him, by the disappointed legatee who wanted Him to interfere in a property dispute, and by the rich young ruler ; by the sanctimonious pillars of orthodoxy, the Pharisees, at the triumphal entry ; by the politicians, the Herodians, who tried to get Him into trouble with Rome ; by the sceptics, the Sadducees, who wanted to make him appear ridiculous over the question of immortality ; and by the men of learning, the Scribes, who, in the end of that day of conflict, admitted He had come through the ordeal well.

" Whence hath this man letters ?   He never was a student."   Look closely at the amazed question. It is not merely Where did He get His wisdom ? Many an unlettered soul has proved himself so apt a scholar in the hard school of experience, as to have earned the title " Sage." Jesus had that wisdom too. But " letters " ?   That was what they could not get over : " a man of letters who had never been to college!"   Their question is an admission. He *had* erudition. How did He come by it ? Galilee in Jesus' day had become practically a bilingual country —the result of the Greek conquest. While Aramaic was Jesus' mother-tongue, it is extremely probable He could converse in Greek also.   For Greeks from beyond the borders of Palestine were attracted by the fame of the prophet. The Syro-Phœnician woman who forced her entreaties on Him by the shores of Tyre, it would appear, spoke Greek (Mark vii. 26). And again when Jesus spoke of going away in a little while, the crowd asked, Will He go to the dispersion among the Greeks ? (John vii. 35), a query which reveals their confidence that He could speak Greek. There is nothing remarkable in the suggestion that Jesus was bilingual.

But Hebrew, the language of the sacred writings had long ceased to be a living language. Jesus' erudition lay in His familiarity with these sacred books. They could, no doubt, be read in Greek, for the Seventy had done their translation in Alexandria. But they were still read in the ancient tongue in the Palestine synagogues, the reader translating the passage into the vernacular as he went along. And did not Jesus once, in the Nazareth synagogue, stand up without any preparation beforehand, and read the passage for the day ? That surely indicates that He was familiar with the ancient tongue. Remember further how frequently He said, " It is written," and how often He challenged His accusers with the query, " What is this that is written ? " or " How readest thou ? " or " Have ye never read ? " and we can have little doubt of His familiarity with the ancient tongue. These are the words of a man sure of His ground, intimately acquainted with the written page to which He referred.

I

And it leads to the first noteworthy general remark about Jesus the Teacher. This Master of religion spoke His message to the world during three short years at the most, and it was after thirty years' preparation. Only he can truly teach who is prepared. Let us dwell for a little on the preparation of the Master Teacher.

Would that we could lift the veil from those hidden years, to see Him at His lessons. Some things we can be certain of, and this above all: it meant weariness, privation, sacrifice. Before He was out of His 'teens, we may conjecture, He followed as chief mourner the mortal remains of Joesph to the grave, and returned to become the bread winner of the home. It left little opportunity for the young lad to carry forward the simple lessons of the village school. One has the strong impression that He spent Himself at the bench, that His brothers might have the fuller education which was denied Him. For from what history tells us of James, it seems probable that he became a learned Pharisee before he met his risen Brother and Lord. There seems to have been a tradition too that Jude had had a good education. One letter of the New Testament has been attributed to him. It is very probable at any rate that James had been sent to Beth-ha-Midrash, the Temple College at Jerusalem. One likes to think that Jesus spent the hours, when the toil of the day was done, learning the ancient tongue, poring over the sacred Scriptures, in order that He might be able to help James and the rest with their lessons while they were at the village school. Now it is not likely that this workman's home possessed copies of all the rolls of the Old Testament, though there may have been one or two. Where did Jesus read them ? We seem to see Him wending His way in the evening twilight to the Synagogue, and begging the Hazzan's permission to read the Synagogue scrolls. What sacred hours these must have been, alone, with the lamp, in the Synagogue, reading and meditating, meditating and reading again.

How much did He know of these ancient Scriptures ? If you study the Gospels in a New Testament that marks the quotations, direct and indirect, from the Old Testament, you will be astonished at the frequency. There are thirty-nine books in the Old Testament, some of them very short, some of minor importance, and not likely to be referred to by Jesus. When one remembers that all that is recorded of the possible three years of the ministry could be compressed into a few weeks, and that even then the record is bare and meagre, it is surely a remarkable fact that He refers to twenty-three or twenty-four of these books in no less than about a hundred instances. If it is so in these parsimonious records, we may well take the liberty to doubt if any part of the Old Testament was left unused by Him in His teaching. Even if there were no further proof, we might have assumed that His Old Testament study had been thorough and complete, for Jesus never did anything slipshod. But some corroborative suggestions may be made. There is one hint that He knew the whole of the Old

Testament from the first book to the last. Call to mind how He refers to the story of the ancient martyrdoms: " From the blood of Abel to the blood of Zecharias who perished between the altar and the Temple." The story of Abel is near the beginning of Genesis, the first book of the Hebrew Bible, and that of Zecharias towards the end of Second Chronicles, the last of the Hebrew Scriptures. Thus, in referring to the long line of martyred lives in the Old Testament, He unhesitatingly names the first and the last recorded. Surely that indicates acquaintance with the whole of the Jewish Scriptures. And there is another hint of it in the way Old Testament language is woven almost unconsciously into the fabric of His speech. When, for example, He pronounced His lamentation over Capernaum, is there no echo of Isaiah's woe on Babylon ? " Thou hast said in thine heart," writes the prophet, " I will ascend into heaven, I will exalt my throne above the stars of God. . . . Yet thou shalt be brought down to Sheol." " And thou, Capernaum," said Jesus, " exalted to heaven wouldst thou be ? Thou shalt be brought down to death."

There is yet another hint of His thoroughness in the fact that the twenty (or thereby) references to Deuteronomy are from all parts of the book, and the score of references to Isaiah shows a similar extensive familiarity. Nay, there is evidence that He read Isaiah, as it now stands in the Jewish Scriptures, from end to end. We recall how the book closes.

Who was Jesus of Nazareth?

Speaking of the world-wide worship of Jehovah that is to be, the prophet closes with a solemn note of judgment upon the wicked: "And they shall go forth and look upon the carcases of the men that have transgressed against me; for their worm shall not die, neither shall their fire be quenched, and they shall be an abhorring unto all flesh." Need we recall how once Jesus used a fragment of that solemn word, with a shudder in His tones: "where their worm dieth not, and their fire is not quenched"?

Let us return for another moment to the Nazareth synagogue, when He stood up to read. The passage for the day was from Isaiah. Recall the words that mark the ending of the reading: "He closed the book." It is one of the few lesser movements that are recorded of Jesus. And the fact that it is there in these parsimonious records means that it was memorable. We watch the crowd listening as the last hushed tones of the Reader's voice dies away. There is a pause of tense silence, every eye fixed on Him, as He rolls the great parchment up, deliberately, precisely, levelling the ends of the scroll with tender care, fastening the thong, and handing it back to the attendant. Neat, and methodical, and thorough in all His ways. We may be sure that the reverence and care with which He handled the book is symbolic of the way in which He studied it. And that careful study is a fact of deep importance. It has often been doubted whether He ever made much of the great dirge of the Suffering Servant in the fifty-third chapter of Isaiah. This fact that He read Isaiah to the very last syllable should help us to believe that He did know it, and that He made it His own. So much for the thoroughness of His preparation.

We cannot forget, however, that Jesus had His favourite passages of Scripture. If Jesus had had a leaved Bible like ours, it would have been easy to find in it the chapters that He loved. That verse in Hosea, for example, would have been deeply underscored, where the prophet puts into the mouth of God: " I will have mercy and not sacrifice." Those personal Psalms, the dearest songs of the humble, covenant-loving folk, the pious in the land, would have been thumb-marked by the frequent handlings. Some pages in the book of Deuteronomy tenderest of all the books of the Law—would almost have fallen open of themselves. For Jesus' reverence for the Scriptures was very different from that of the Scribes. The Massoretes regarded each letter with a superstitious sacrosanctity. They worked in fear and trembling, not daring to alter a jot or tittle, even where these were obviously wrong. They wiped their pens and took a fresh dip of ink, each time they wrote God's name. Before they would even open the book to read or write they washed ceremonially and said a prayer. The doctrine of plenary inspiration is Jewish, not Christian. Jesus would have none of it. He did have a deep and tender reverence for the Scriptures, but His reverence did not prevent a fearless freedom in the handling of them. Nothing was final or eternal to Him that did not commend itself as Divine in His own illumined conscience. In the name of the Divine law of nature, planted in the hearts of the parents of the race, He set aside the Mosaic Law, where it was only a compromise because of the hardness of men's hearts. He went behind the forbidding externality of the Decalogue to the higher law of the inner motive. Unless that was right, the spirit of the Law was broken, however much the letter might be kept. He set aside the wild, vindictive justice of " An eye for an eye " for the nobler law of retaliation in love. Ceremonial law, again, must, in His judgment, give way to the law of man's fundamental needs. He disconcerted the Rabbis by thrusting the conduct of their sacrosanct King David before them, as a law-breaker whose action He approved. Solomon was to them the type of wisdom. But to Jesus the babes in earthly wisdom were better than he. Solomon fills a great and glittering place in their sacred history. Jesus has for all time set that glory in its proper place. It is surpassed by the lily of the field.

Indeed, judging by the Old Testament illustrations that He chose, it was not the so-called great movements of history, the supposed pomp and glitter of war, that appealed to Him. From the hills that surrounded Nazareth He had often looked down on the great plain of Esdraelon, and seen the place where Sisera was overwhelmed in the torrents of

Kishon, the mountains of Gilboa where Saul and Jonathan fell, the valley down which Gideon chased the Midianites, and the peak of Carmel where Elijah's altar smoked. But He passed it all by. It was another kind of event which appealed to Him— Abel murdered because his sacrifice was accepted by God, Noah warned of God, Abraham the friend of God, Lot fleeing at God's summons from the wicked cities, Jacob's vision of God at Bethel, and at Peniel, Moses' vision of God at the bush, Elijah used of God at Zarephath, Elisha and the heathen Naaman, Michaiah the son of Imlah heroically rebuking Ahab in the name of God, Jonah preaching God's judgment to Nineveh; most of them instances of the mysterious drawing near of God to men.

Thus, if we have yet to learn the lesson of Jesus' freedom in the handling of the Old Testament, His genius in selection might well be studied with profit too, in our efforts to impart religious knowledge to others. Learned Jewish scholars sometimes accuse Jesus of borrowing all His best thoughts from the Old Testament and the Talmud. Jesus would not be greatly concerned to repudiate the impeachment. " Every scribe instructed unto the Kingdom is like a householder bringing out his of treasure-house old things as well as new." But the instructive thing for us is to witness how He makes the old new by setting them in true perspective. And we are reminded of Wellhausen's notable reply to this

Jewish insinuation. You will find much of the Sermon on the Mount, perhaps, in the ancient Jewish writings, but how much more besides! One golden sentence is often lost in the dreary desert of dry and barren pages. The great glory of Jesus the Teacher is that He rediscovered those gems and flowers and carried them back into the common ways of men. Only the eye of genius can find these immortal treasures and set them in the light where their true significance is seen.

II

Let us look at a few which form the main features of the lesson He taught to men. Who but the Master could have selected, and in selecting summed up the whole Mosaic Law, in the two commandments which He called the greatest : Love God with all your heart and mind and soul and strength ; love your neighbour as yourself. It was from the book of the Law that the first religious lessons of the young Jesus were learned—the austere majesty of the One true God, and the solemn mountain-heights of the commandments. He not only mastered these, but His keen mind went searching further and further into them. Jesus was a great questioner as a boy. Probably nobody ever became a great teacher who was not a great questioner in his youth. Jesus was what Scottish people mistakenly call an old-fashioned child. He

was as fond of the company of grown-ups as He was
of His companions ; He was always plying the grey-
beards with questions. The time He was lost in
Jerusalem, He wandered into the House of the
Midrash, and soon made Himself quite at home
among the learned professors, and began His old
ploy of questioning them. We are told they were
astonished at His answers. We imagine they were
quite as much astonished at His questions. No, He
was not old-fashioned ; it is always the clear-eyed
simplicity of the child that asks the deepest questions.
And it was because He found an outlet for His
questions by consorting with old men in childhood
that his Heart remained young enough in later life
to be the companion of children, the great Teacher
of the simple. All the majesty of Moses' Law is
reduced to very simple terms in those two greatest
commandments : Love God better than your best
self ; love your neighbour as yourself. Nevertheless
they are deep as life is deep, and high as heaven is
high. The heart of all the Law is Love. That was
the first part of the Master Teacher's lesson. It
was " a brilliant flash of the highest religious genius,"
says Mr. C. G. Montefiore.

But though the picture of the austere, law-loving
God of Sinai was among the earliest of His impressions, we do not believe He suffered the fate of so
many of His day, and felt God far away—a mere
rumour hidden behind the Law. In the hushed
awe of His mother's voice, and the solemn tenderness

of her face, when she taught Him in the home, He must have felt God near. He may often have heard the synagogue preachers say, " Wherever two sit down to meditate upon the Law, the Shechinah of God is with them." And the young heart, full of the sacred talks at His mother's knee, could have bowed His assent to that. The Shechinah of God— the sacred shining of the Unseen Face ! And those early impressions woke a longing for a nearer and clearer fellowship, which was not stayed till it was satisfied to the full. Sometime about His twelfth year, we know from the word He spoke to His mother in the Temple, the greatest secret of His life dawned on Him at last. God was His Father ! Yes, you may find that word too in the Old Testament, if you care. But here at any rate nothing could be less like a lesson learned by rote by Jesus. It was a sacred fact which He had found true in His own experience. He became the great Teacher because He taught from the heart. And He taught from the heart because the Divine light had shined there. This was the supreme lesson He taught to men: God is your Father because I know He is Mine. It is the greatest of the gems this highest Explorer of the Unseen carried back from the desert of prosing and quibbling and hairsplitting created by the Scribes ; the greatest splendour He set shining forever in the heart of our humanity. If the inner secret of the Law— love to God and man—was the first part of the lesson He learned and taught, the second and greatest was

the Father who sees in secret and rewards in secret.
And under God, not the law-book, but the Psalms,
we imagine,—these favourite songs of His—were His
tutors—rather, we should say, the voices by which
He found expression for the great experience when it
came. "When I consider the heavens, the work of
Thy fingers, the moon and the stars which Thou
hast ordained, what is man that Thou art mindful
of him, or the son of man that Thou visitest him?"
Son of man was the designation He gave Himself.
It may not be altogether wrong to suppose it was due,
in the first instance, to the association of that Psalm
with His great experience.

And this paved the way for the third great lesson
He taught to men. If God is the Father of mankind,
then every man is our brother ; we are all one family.
It was a lesson that brought pain to Him. For He
could not help seeing how little men did to prove
it true. Life was unlovely—full of passion, bitterness, strife, estrangement : men hurt each other so.
And because He did not find the fact of brotherhood
on earth, it became His dream—a shining ideal to be
made true some day. And here the ancient prophetic
writings began to comfort Him. They were His
tutors now. They foretold this dream of a Divine
Kingdom to be established on earth, when God's will
would be obeyed in love. And it grew from less to
more in the prophets : first a dim, broken, and
imperfect thing, narrow, exclusive, national, with
cries of vengeance in it. Then Amos came declaring

the God of righteousness to be the God of all the world, not of the Jews alone; and Hosea, revealing Him as God of the home, a tender, forgiving God; then Ezekiel and Jeremiah, revealing God as calling to individual responsibility, until the Realm of God grew holy, personal, and near. It was the will of God obeyed in individual hearts. The Kingdom is within. This was the third gem Jesus rescued from the vindictiveness and doom and judgment that hid it from sight. If the inner secret of the moral law was Love, if behind the law was the God whose name is Father, which means Love, then coming some day upon the earth was the Kingdom of Love, where God's law of love would be obeyed in love by men.

But how to make men obedient, how to bring them God's forgiveness, how to unite them to each other by reconciling them to God—that was the last great problem that weighed on the young Man of Nazareth's soul. And in answer to it He began to hear another note in the prophets, which was echoed as a broken sigh in the blind hearts of the people of His day. Some one was coming. A Deliverer was coming—soon, soon. Would that he were here! A warrior king to rescue them from oppression, and restore the ancient throne of David. That was how He heard it first, and heard it most frequently, for it was thus the popular hope had shaped itself. But to Jesus' mind the picture did not blend with the law of Love, nor yet with His

experience of the God of Love; it struck a discord
in the ideal of the Kingdom of Love. And there
were holier things spoken in the Scriptures, of God's
Anointed, God's Messiah. It was that truer note
that most appealed to Him in the ancient prophecies.
For Love lives to serve. The God of Love is the
chief servant of His world. And God's Anointed
must be God's great Servant upon earth. Then an
unknown prophet of the exile saw the full vision at
last. Love's holiest service lies in suffering and
sacrifice. God's Anointed must be God's Suffering
Servant. That prophecy wakened no response in
the heart of Israel till Jesus came. But there can be
no doubt it is echoed again and again in Jesus' speech.
This was the last great flower He rescued from the
desert of Israel's dreary past—the crimson flower of
sacrifice. And when He saw the crowds swaying
and trembling beneath the fiery Baptiser's preaching,
when He witnessed the great repentance-movement
at the Jordan, the hour, He felt, had struck: He
solemnly dedicated Himself in baptism to the great
task for God, of suffering, service, sacrifice.

A Law of Love, a God of Love, a Kingdom of
Love, and a Sacrifice of Love that the Kingdom
might come true: that was the Master Teacher's
message, the lesson He taught to the world, a message
whose burden the Teacher came Himself at last
to be regarded. Nicodemus had spoken truer
than he thought when he said, " Thou art a Teacher
come from God." " Come from God "—yes,

these words constitute the sacred credentials of His calling as a Teacher.

III

We have spoken of the Master Teacher's preparation to teach, and of the lesson He taught to men. We would fain speak also of the method of the Master Teacher. His one great principle as a Teacher—and it is the true ideal of all religious teaching—was just to let sanctified personality do its perfect work. The deep things of God cannot be communicated in any other way. We debate much about the place of the religious lesson in schools ; it is even more important that we should have religious teachers. It is not information, details, mere dry facts, it is a life we have to impart in religious teaching. The information must glow with emotion, the details be lit with central significance, the facts be made alive. And that can only be done by sanctified personality. " For their sakes I sanctify Myself," Jesus said. Not "For their sakes I organise a school," nor yet " For their sakes I draw up a scheme of lessons." Christ's first word in teaching is *character*, and the second is *love*. Love has its watchword : " For their sakes " ; and character its command : " sanctify thyself."

What then was the nature of the influence of Christ's sanctified personality upon those who listened to Him ? How did it work ? The questions are almost foolish. Who can tell exactly ? Who can

48

explain the subtle ways by which Christ draws near to men ? We may analyse as we like. It is only the outer accompaniments we are dealing with.

There must have been some subtle power in the quality of Christ's voice, for example. He did not strive nor cry, neither did men hear Him shouting on the streets. There was absolutely nothing of the loud-mouthed, blustering demagogue about Him. His was a quiet voice—serene, and clear, and convincing, like light; floating down from the heights of His own rapt communion with God, like the sound of Cathedral bells at evensong, rousing the hearts of men to the highest, holiest thoughts of which they were capable; a magnetic voice, arresting, commanding, thrilling, penetrating, holding all the notes of the still, sad music of humanity, transmuted in the ethereal tones of heaven—the sound of many waters.

And the face must have had much to do with it. According to tradition, it was a face which they who look on it can both love and fear. It was a face that enthralled men, yet haunted them. Some ineffable purity about it set it far away from the mean and dusty ways of men—disconcerting, searching, judging purity. And yet—there were those dark, mysterious shadows gathering beneath the love-lighted eyes— burning compassion which brought His far-off purity down into the midst of our humanity, sharing our brokenness, bearing our griefs, carrying our sorrows, and our sins—taking to do with that in which He had no guilty partnership. Holiness and love—these are the two supreme attributes of God. And the souls of men, as they stood in His presence, woke up and cried in adoring wonder, " God! We see God in Him—the light of the knowledge of the glory of God in the face of Jesus Christ."

Mannerisms too in their own way convey personality. And Jesus had some such marks by which men knew Him. That frequent word of emphasis, for example : " Verily, I say unto you "— in one form or other it is found over eighty times on Jesus' lips. His " verily " was a deed which made men's doubts and questionings and fears fall at their feet as dead. Recall also the impressive pause He often made before He spoke. Some gift of personality was communicated in those speaking silences ; as if He were beckoning men into the holy place, as if He were reminding them "The Lord is in His holy temple : let all the earth keep silence before Him." Remember again that frequent, long, still gaze of His into the faces of His hearers. A mannerism, a gesture of the Teacher's, arresting attention, it was a symbol of one of the most significant facts of His personality —the way He had of losing Himself, becoming absorbed in the needs, the longings, the tragic stories which He saw on their faces as on an open page. Like the true teacher, He wanted to know completely those whom He would teach.

A crowd was never a mass of units to Him. He

was always individualising, singling people out,
dealing with them heart to heart. When He spoke
to the crowd each man thought He was speaking to
him. Many of the greatest things He ever said
were spoken actually to individuals : His word to
Peter, for example, " The gates of hell shall not
prevail against My Church"; to the dry-as-parch-
ment old professor, reluctant to put away his pride
and become a scholar, a child at Jesus' feet, " Ye
must be born again "; to the jaded profligate at
the well, " God is Spirit "; to Simon the Pharisee,
" To whom little is forgiven the same loveth little ";
to the tempting lawyer, the parable of the Good
Samaritan ; to the rich young ruler, " There is none
good but One—God "; to Martha, " I am the
Resurrection and the Life "; to Thomas, " I am the
Way"; to Philip, "He that hath seen Me hath seen
the Father "; to Pilate, " My Kingdom is not of
this world "; to the dying thief, " To-day shalt
thou be with Me in Paradise." There is a whole
compendium of theology in these utterances.

And yet there is a remarkable detachedness about
most of His sayings. That is another characteristic
of the supreme Teacher, His unobtrusiveness. He
never forces Himself into unwilling company, or
unwilling minds. It was not His way to worry
or terrify men into religion by questioning them
insistently about their souls. There is about Him a
delicacy, a reverence for the sacrosanctity of
personality. If the religious life is to mean the

highest and best for man or child, it must not be thrust into a violated soul ; it must steal its way gently in by the opened gates of humility and love. And this explains in part too His practice of telling stories, parables. Of course the main reason for this picturesque way of conveying truth is to make the truth vivid and real. " Truth embodied in a tale may enter in by lowly doors." But there is another reason why Jesus and all the great teachers of religion have used the parabolic method. It is because they sometimes have a message too terrible for men to be directly confronted with it. It is in the obliquely held mirror that a man sees the aspects of himself he is too apt to ignore. Jesus spoke with authority, but He hardly ever used the tone of peremptoriness. He seldom said, " You must do this," and never said, " You must not do that." To hedge a young mind about with a thorny fence of " don'ts " may make him docile and disciplined, but it makes him a mechanical soul. Jesus took the way of showing men the reasonableness of His view of life and His way of life. He had faith in the human mind, He respected human responsibility. And it all comes back to this. He had confidence in the power of the teacher's sanctified personality to make its influence tell in its own unobtrusive way on the souls of those who listened.

And because He was always more concerned to find an effective way of approach than to force an entrance on the soul, His art as a teacher was

concentrated on that.   Consider the opportunism of
the supreme Teacher, the way He had of seizing on
circumstance and incident in the life and scenes
around Him.   On many an occasion when He said
" Behold," He must have called attention to something visible or audible : to the sower striding down
the fields with swinging hands, to the rustling of the
wind in the trees and the reeds, to the birds of the
air, to the lilies of the field, to the city on the hill,
and to the fields ripening for harvest.   And He
always took men as He found them.   To the thirsty
soul at the well He offered the living water ; among
life's broken folk He called Himself the Physician ;
to the country pilgrims at the feast He said, " I am
the good shepherd " ; to the hungry multitudes,
" I am the bread of life."   We miss the concreteness,
the vividness of much that He said by failing to
visualise the actual scene in which it was spoken.
There is a story told of a powerful address delivered
by the great Whitefield once at Cambuslang, when
he seized on the phases of a passing thunderstorm
with telling effect.   He was afterwards asked to
publish the address.   " I have no objection," he
replied, " if you will print the lightning, the thunder
and the rainbow with it."   You can't convey these
things on paper.   That is perhaps why the only
thing that Jesus ever wrote, so far as the Gospels
record, was a word or two in the dust of the Temple
court, something that the next gust of wind swirled
out.   The power of utilising the occasion is one of

the marks of a great personality. And in Jesus it is surely supreme.

Think further of His humour, His genial irony. We are now getting past the day when men believed that the Man of Sorrows never laughed or smiled. The Gospel pages sparkle with His humour—another of His methods of breaking down barriers reared against the truth. He surely smiled when He contrasted men with sparrows, the guttersnipes of the bird world, and with sheep, the most common of all God's common beasts; when He heard the sycophant courtiers calling some tyrant potentate by the obsequious name " Euergetes," though they cursed behind his back; when He compared the Pharisees, so stiff and proper that it sounds almost like an accusation to suggest that they had ever been young, to children playing at weddings and funerals in the market place. He surely smiled when He witnessed His mother's half-laughing vexation at her own foolishness, when one of the children came home with the new patch she had sown on the old coat hanging by a thread, and the hole bigger than ever; when He saw the man with the rueful face looking at his old, cracked wineskin that had burst and let all the wine run out—the good new wine; when He said to a few fishermen, " Come and fish for men "; when He looked on the Syrophœnician woman and said it would not be right to give the children's bread to the " doggies," and listened to her witty retort; when He passed the derelict house,

half-built, and learned it was because the builder's
bank account had been wound up prematurely;
when He heard of the king who had gone to war
with a contemptible little army, and was compelled
to patch up an ignominious peace before he reached
the battle-field. To say that Jesus did not smile on
these occasions is to put too great a tax on one's
credulity. Surely there is humour in the idea of
trying to fatten one's pigs for market with a bucket
of pearls; in the fantastic picture of a camel trying
to shove itself through the eye of a needle; in the
picture of a man complacently handing a stone to the
child who had asked for bread; of the family sitting
solemnly round an inverted tub from beneath which
a feeble gleam or two of lamp-light is struggling; of
folk out searching bramble-bushes for grapes, or
hunting among the thistles on the moors for figs;
of the man with the plank in his eye tenderly
solicitous over his brother who has got a speck of
sawdust in his; of the Pharisee with a trumpeter
heralding his progress down the street while he
distributes his little doles, tremendously in love with
himself; of another Pharisee straining out the
daddy-long-legs from his wine, yet swallowing a
camel, monstrous daddy-long-legs, hump, and pads,
and sardonic smile as well.

In some of the parables again there is a touch of
sheer and obvious fun. There is the sleepy father,
in bed with his children, crying, " I can't get up; the
door is barred long since "—as if it were any harder

to unbar at midnight than at sunset, or sunrise. "And my children are with me in bed "—as if he were unwilling to make a fuss and waken them, and yet he was shouting through the room to a man outside the door in the dark street. One little pair of ears at least were once awakened in Nazareth and heard. There is the factor who had just got notice to quit, out trying to secure a soft bed for himself, prudent man, by being kind to some of his master's debtors—at his master's expense. There is the hard judge who thought himself a terrible fellow, always talking to himself, trying to make your flesh creep: "What do I care for men ? . . . God ! Who is afraid of God ? Not me—an atheist ! " Yet he shrugs his shoulders in ridiculous self-pity at the strident tongue of a widow woman, afraid it would end in her giving him two black eyes ! It is Jesus' description, certainly not of God, but of unfaith's gloomy notion of God.

And this great Teacher, who could thus dissolve the ice of inaccessibility in the alembic of laughter, was all the time a heart brimming over with sympathy and compassion, a longing to give Himself to men—personality too big to be kept to itself. "Full of grace and truth," John says. And grace is just the overflow of large-hearted personality. The Teacher Himself was the lesson, His own best gift to men—giving Himself at last on a Cross that the imprisoning fetters around our human nature might be broken and that we might be set free.

The Master Teacher

"He taught no doctrine that was not part of Himself; He revealed a life in God that can only be won by us through a life in Christ."

Here is the comfort for every teacher of Divine things. It is not ourselves we have to give to those we teach, it is Him. We do well to imitate His methods, where we can. But the best we can do in our preparation is to keep close to Him. That is how "for their sakes" we may "sanctify ourselves." He chose Twelve, we are told, not that He might instruct them in a long and strenuous course of study, but just that they might be with Him. We can learn of Him as these unlettered men did. He Himself is the Bread of Life. He came not to communicate the stony diet of philosophy, but to offer food of angels, soul satisfaction, placing it within reach of every hungry soul.

"How much of the sea can a child carry in its hands?" asks Samuel Rutherford. "As little," he adds, "do I take away of Thee, my great sea, my boundless and running over Christ Jesus." Yes, but the water in the child's hand is of the same essential nature as the ocean depths. And the water Christ gives is living water, ever replenishing and renewing itself. We must keep close to Him. We must drink, and again drink of the life-giving stream of His personality. And men and little ones will take knowledge of us that we have been with Jesus; they will learn of Him, they will receive Him, through us. It was in an intimacy it began. It is in an intimacy it goes on forever. " I am come," He said in deep emotion once, " to cast fire upon the earth. Would it were already burning ! " It is the fire that burns on the altar of His heart, that kindles the torch of every sanctified life, and touches to flame the waiting sacrifice in the hearts of young and old.

III

The Tragic Schism : Can it be Healed?

CHRISTIANITY gathers round one central *fact* of history—the deed of Divine Forgiveness. The meaning of this fact spreads out until it is lost to human view in the far distances of eternity. The recognition of this has often led sincere souls— it led Coleridge—to say that it must simply be accepted. It is a mystery; but *factum est,* and that ought to content us.

Yet the soul accepting is surely the soul in some measure understanding. There is a difference between the mystery which is an impenetrable horror of great darkness, and the mystery that is a vast, luminous orb at the centre of which you one day find yourself—an orb of light shot through and through on every hand with rainbow harmonies. Christianity's central fact is in reality the most familiar and the most moving of human experiences—transfigured in the light of heaven. It is a mystery simply because its meaning cannot be exhausted by human description. It is exhaustless as the mind and heart of God. It is the mind and heart of God.

No man can stand to view the wide horizons of the Divine Heart without being conscious that his feet are on holy ground. Yet God does not bid us veil our eyes. It is no part of a genuine piety to do so. And, though we cannot hope ' *in hoc vastum pelagus divinitatis navigare*,' we can learn something of the wonder of the ocean where the sun glints on the limpid, green depths of the waves by the shore—perhaps even in the whisper of the shell.

I

The deepest yearning of the human soul arises from *the sense of the absence of God*. The quest of Religion is to reach communion with God. When we take a bird's-eye view of the long panorama of evolution, we see nature operating through her patient laws to " break, bloom, and blossom " at last into individuality. The true reading of the world reveals it as wholly given over to individuality. And this last result of the evolutionary process betrays its final source. The effect cannot be greater than its source. Its origin is the heart of an infinite spiritual Life. If the end of Creation is a society of individuals, then—speaking in the language of religion—the ground of Creation must have been the loneliness of God. This was the Divine Purpose—to produce a race of self-conscious beings—a kingdom of souls who should, by a life of moral effort and aspiration here, become fit for perfect communion with God. The screen of Nature and her slow-moving laws was His method of separating off such centres of personal life from the infinite Life. " So exquisite is the delicacy of His non-obtrusion, so subtly sensitive is the Glory that conceals itself, that He withdraws behind the veil of Nature and the operations of the mind and the ordinary movements of life, to give us the power of standing at a certain distance from Him, that we may contemplate and converse with Him, or, if we will, misdeem and forsake Him for a season." The gift of spiritual freedom, moral consciousness, is God's way of entrusting to us a share in the fashioning of ourselves—for Him. Here, in man, the Divine Spirit immanent in Creation is reaching back to complete the circle of the creative process in personal fellowship with the personal God.

But if God is a personal and transcendent Being, then the yearning in the heart of man—which is the immanent Divine Spirit, groaning in Creation to reach back to the heart of God—is not the only spiritual activity at work to complete the circle of creative purpose. The heart of God is also engaged in a search, by personal ways, to reach us from above—in grace.

Once, in time, the circle was completed, when the Nazareth Boy, in the hour of moral maturity, surrendered Himself in perfect trust to this seeking Grace Divine, without any intervening period of failure, or sense of estrangement, or moral wretchedness ; when " the Son " whispered with unclouded consciousness into the listening silence of Eternity the mystic name, " My Father."

Who was Jesus of Nazareth?

If there is any other sinless soul among mankind, let him make the same claim. For the mass of mankind, moral consciousness begins with a feeling of disharmony, of inner estrangement, a sense of the absence of God. There may be many degrees of need for forgiveness among men, but the gracious, forth-flowing impulse of the Heart of God, seeking from above for men, is received by all but the sinless in an experience of forgiveness.

Where shall we look for the Hand of God thrust through the Unseen in reconciling love, if not in Him in whom the circle of Creation was perfectly completed : in Him of whom alone the Spirit could say, "This is My beloved Son in whom I am well-pleased " ?

II

It is with this " tragic schism " we are here concerned—this misunderstanding and estrangement between the soul of man and God ; this " sense of the absence of God " as we have described it, so as to include all phases of the guilt-consciousness. And the problem—for God and for men—is how to turn the estrangement into friendship. What is it that takes place in that profound and moving moral experience, with which, in a broken and imperfect way, human nature is so pathetically familiar ?

Must man do anything himself to bring the misunderstanding to an end ? Can he make any reparation for the offence that lies at the root of

the estrangement ? Can the offender be the healer ?
Would anything that he could do to end the breach
satisfy himself in the first place ; but, above all,
would it satisfy God ?

Let us imagine a case of broken confidence
between two human friends. You are the offender,
let us say, and a very dear and valued friend the
offended one. You know you are the offender.
You feel you ought to take the initiative. Your
conscience is reproaching you. What sort of
reconciliation will satisfy that conscience of yours ?
You set about trying to undo the wrong. Suppose
you succeeded perfectly. (Or—no ! that is impossible. You may make good material loss or injury,
but you can never wholly undo a wrong ; indeed,
in a sense you can never undo the smallest jot or
tittle of a wrong for the real wrong is a spiritual
thing. Between you and the old glad past of
perfect confidence a blinding rain, a mist of suspicion
and distrust has fallen, and things can never, with
that memory behind, be quite the same again.)
But suppose you had succeeded in paying back in
full, so far as outward action can pay back, for all
the damage done. And then, in the next place—
for the real injury is the wound to friendship—
suppose you came to your friend, and tried to undo
that by confessing in sorrow, bitter and sincere,
that you were wrong. Penitence has done its utmost.
Is the wound healed, the reconciliation completed ?
. . . What of your friend ?

Who was Jesus of Nazareth?

Suppose your friend had just accepted your action, passively, silently, as a matter of course. Would you be quite content to call that a reconciliation? Would you not rather be inclined to come home and, shutting yourself in your room, say to yourself, in a flood of bitter weeping, " For all that *I* have done we are as far apart as ever " ?

There is a paradox here, but it is a real fact of experience and we must acknowledge it. The paradox is, that though you, the offender, feel that the reparation is yours to make good, yet the making good by outward deed and inward penitence—if that were all—would never satisfy you that a reconciliation had been brought about. It takes two to effect a reconciliation. *The offended one, also, must pass through an experience that is the complement and counterpart of all the bitter sorrow that you, the offender, have undergone in your effort after restoration.*

What, then, is it that must happen in the offended one's heart? Suppose we represent the offended one as breaking through the silence of the first encounter and offering you a bare acknowledgment of your efforts. Would you be satisfied? Your friend has held out his hand to you, but quite coldly, and in a voice of stony indifference said, " Well, well; let by-gones be by-gones. I forgive you." Would you be quite happy again? Would you not go home almost more miserable than before? The touch of that cold hand only repelled you, and you shrank within yourself. There was *no* reconciliation worthy the name.

There is a striking illustration in Mrs. Humphry Ward's *The Marriage of William Ashe*. It is the story of a rising young politician who is almost certain of the Premiership some day. He marries a young, winsome, but wayward wife—dashing, volatile, restless, unconventional, with a strain of French blood in her veins. She does things so shockingly outrageous to the society in which she is obliged to move because of her husband's position, that she well-nigh ruins his career. But again and again there is a reconciliation, and a fresh start made. She was never truly repentant; and at last she commits the grave sin of deserting him for another. Her fit of wayward caprice is soon over, and she repents, at length, in all the terrible bitterness of that word. Alas! that is, when all is said, the best, the only, undoing of a wrong that mortal man can make; and what a tragic penalty a real repentance is! She sends and tells her husband; there is a sincere and childlike candour about her confession. From the wilderness of this heart in extreme bitterness the great call comes to the man— to forgive. What will the cost of a true forgiveness be for him? Will a mere word do? If he would take his wife to his heart again, he must surrender all —honour, and the fame of public service, the loftiest post in the land, the infinite riches of his life—for love. Society will certainly cast him off if he stoops

to associate himself with her once more. . . .
He writes to her. He *says* he forgives her ; he will
make provision for her. But she is surely too
sensible to think he can ever make her again what
she once was to him. That is the burden of his
letter, and it simply makes the poor, broken heart
bleed afresh. Womanly intuition—nay, the human
heart in her—tells her there is no reconciliation,
no real forgiveness there ; and she will not come
home, though there is nothing but death before
her. The rich young ruler of this modern story
realised that the call to forgive meant, " Sell all
that thou hast "—all thy dear-won social and
political position. And the cost was too much for
him. He went away sorrowful.

Yes, it is easy to say, " I forgive "—and often very
cheap. But if there is to be a genuine reconciliation, it is not merely the sinner, the offender, that
has (in Bushnell's phrase) " to make cost." Repentance there must be, of course ; but the only forgiveness that will satisfy the sinner is the forgiveness
that comes through fire and water, out of the very
depths of the heart of the wronged one, charged
with all the tragedy of the wrong. Only forgiveness
laden with the agony of the offence can be experienced by the wrong-doer as real forgiveness—can
bring perfect assurance of restoration to the guilty
soul.

The Tragic Schism : Can it be Healed?

III

Is it then humanly possible to heal the mis-understanding between man and God ? What is the extent of our offence against God ? We have to remember here that the depth of our offence, our guilt, is measured not by what we think of it, but by what God thinks of it. Sin has sometimes been defined as selfishness. The definition is not without its usefulness, but it is only a weighing of sin in a human balance, not in God's balance. We do not see all our sinfulness by simply taking into account our relations with our fellow-men : we must try to see ourselves in the light of the purity of the Holy God with whom we have to do. Even of our most secret and private sins the question is, "What has God to say ? "

The moral and spiritual world has a law of gravitation of its own. Every particle of matter in the universe exerts an influence on every other, to the remotest star in the furthest bounds of space. Not a stone falls but *some* change, however infin-itesimally small, takes place in the arrangement of the forces of the Universe. It is the same in con-duct. "The evil that I did," says Dr. Horton, "passed out into the Universe with an influence the extent of which I can never measure, and the force of which I can never arrest. Just as pulsing out from our sun goes the light which is reaching the nearest fixed star in the Centaur after three-and-a-half years' travelling, and then will go on and on reaching different systems years and centuries after, so the sin I committed was as a little ray of lurid light : it passed out into an infinite Universe, travelled, and is travelling, on and on and on. I can never arrest it and I can never undo it. It is done, and it is attached to me, the doer, forever."

The same writer instances the undertone of melancholy which ran through the preaching of John Donne, the eloquent Elizabethan divine—melancholy which betrayed the conviction that the licentious poems of his early, unconverted days would live to corrupt and taint young lives, centuries after his eloquent tongue was silent. He had had a glimpse of what his sin meant in the eyes of God.

> Action is transitory—a step, a blow,
> A movement of a muscle this way or that ;
> 'Tis done, and in the after vacancy
> We wonder at ourselves as men betrayed.

Man's life is woven into the warp and woof of existence. Not a step can he take but it is caught up by this web of life, and " is bent into directions and produces events which take place inevitably and without regard to our desires or regrets."[1] Our smallest act lets loose some moral impulse for good or evil which vibrates to the end of the Universe. Our tiniest act of sin creates a discord which goes shuddering through all the soul of God. For the laws by which the Universe is upheld have their source and life in the character of God. The

[1] A. C. Bradley, in *Shakespearean Tragedy.*

moral basis and the cosmic conditions of Divine forgiveness are one and the same.   In the eyes of All-holy Omniscience, individual guilt must be swathed in cosmic gloom.

Taking our stand upon the Pantheism of Paul, let us try to express this in a picture which, however crudely materialistic in itself, may yet be a shadow of the truth. " God," says Paul, " is in all, and through all, and over all "; " of Him, and through Him, and to Him are all things "; " of Him are all things, and we in Him "; " in Him we live, and move, and have our being."   Creation, in Goethe's phrase, is " the living garment of Deity."   " God is in the city "—that is a familiar mode of speech with us : it is still truer and more heart-searching to say, " The city is in God."   We often speak of the Spirit of God moving through the valleys and plains with their burthen of teeming human life : it is still truer to say that the communities of the valleys are like nerve-tracks lying along the breast of God. A sordid sin takes place in some populous valley. The news sweeps from end to end in a little, hustling, hurrying breeze of gossip, moving the cynical to laughter, the vulgar to filthy talk, the decent to a shrinking shame, and those whom it most nearly concerns to a bitterness as of death itself.   The moral tone of the valley is lowered, its life depressed, by it.   Some soul, a life-cell in that nerve-track, has gone wrong, and created a discord which jars through the entire length of it : an exquisite agony of quivering pain, which registers itself in the soul of God! The moral filth and slime of cities— fester-spots; the red wound of war across a continent—causing a deep, shuddering horror, or reflected as a great redness of shame, in the holy heart and soul of God! God is a great, throbbing, sensitive, tender Heart of Love in which the failure, sin, and shame of man *lives*—beats—burns. The eyes of guilt look up and call it "Wrath."

> I heard a voice upon the slope
> Cry to the summit, "Is there any hope?"
> To which an answer pealed from that high land,
> But in a tongue no man could understand;
> And on the glimmering limit far withdrawn
> God made Himself an awful rose of dawn.

IV

Does it not seem, then, that this misunderstanding between man and his Maker is too great to be healed? If in a case of separation between human friends it is impossible for the wrong-doer to pay down in full for all the damage done, and completely undo the wrong, how much less possible is it for the wrong-doer to do anything to restore the broken relation, when the case is between man and God? Our sins are discords which go jangling through all the ordered harmony of the world, and are therefore injuries to God. As Anselm puts it, the smallest sin is an insult to the Supreme Being. It is therefore an infinite insult; therefore something not to be committed to save worlds from perdition. Though we possessed a world—nay, many worlds—and offered them all to God in atonement for sin, they would be insufficient. Further, just because we have sinned, and thus blunted the conscience, because we are finite and ignorant, we cannot realise the extent and depth of our sin, and therefore cannot feel a penitent sorrow for our offence that could be anything like the measure of the wound it has caused to God's holy love. Only an Infinite Being, One greater than all worlds, can repair an infinite insult. Only the infinitely holy heart of an All-seeing God can feel the full pain and horror of man's sin against Him. We *ought* to make reparation, but only God *can*. That is the tragedy of sin. Is it, then, possible to repair the breach ? It is not possible—unless God does it.

Has God done it ? Can we be certain that God has reckoned and paid down all the infinite cost which the forgiving heart of the wronged one alone can and must pay, if there is to be a perfect reconciliation ? Can we be assured that God's forgiveness has come to us, out of a heart that has laboured with an agony deeper than all the infamy of human sin ? To that question we must next address ourselves. The answer can be stated here in a single word—*Christ*. That Life of tragic sorrow was the cost of forgiveness to God. The Cross was God's heart broken at length in His effort to give Himself again to the being who had caused the terrible estrangement. The more we gaze on that Crucified One, the more certain do we grow that it is not in hell that all the agony of all the world is felt. It is in the heart of God. It is only there. And " there is none other name under heaven given among men, whereby we must be saved."

The Tragic Schism : Has it been Healed?

IT is the legitimate boast of the literature of to-day that never before have the intricacies of the human soul received so subtle and so thorough an investigation. None of the spiritual lights and shadows, none of the great emotions and crises of the soul are thought to have escaped its searching pen. Yet in the case of the experience of forgiveness literary analysis has largely failed. It has failed to understand, or fully to evaluate, the moral passion which true forgiveness demands of the forgiving heart. We have had many moving pictures of the passion of a soul repentant, but few of the passion of a soul forgiving. There is a pathos about the failure. Because we are human we understand something of what it means to repent. Because we are human we have seldom guessed what it costs to forgive. And this, in spite of the fact that the sincerity of a real repentance refuses to be satisfied with an unreal forgiveness—the cold forgiveness that has issued from a soul unshaken.

It is self-interest, pride, concern for personal dignity, self-esteem which make the business of forgiving most irksome to men. And the broken-hearted penitent has usually to be content with the human forgiveness that has meant the breaking with these things. Nevertheless this scarcely touches the central problem of forgiveness. Forgiveness is a summons to love. The moral energy and effort required in forgiving is the greatest drain that can be made upon the passion of love. And it is true love—love without fleck or stain of self—that understands this best. But perfect love exists only in the absolutely pure in heart—in God. It is holiness—the very ground of love, the sense of the awful difference between right and wrong—which makes forgiveness God's most arduous task. Holiness cannot stoop to condone a violation of its life and law—that would be to undo Creation's bands. And forgiveness is Holy Love somehow taking to do with sin.

Yet this task, which well-nigh exhausts the limits of Divine possibility, is precisely that which God cannot help doing. Self-sacrifice, the ideal goal of all human morality, must be the very inmost essence of all the Divine activity. And Forgiveness is the supreme opportunity for self-sacrifice. For Forgiveness is what heals the broken peace and concord of that society of souls which is to become the Kingdom of God. Holy Love alone can know the cost of this. But Holy Love does not count the cost. It *pays* the cost. It was in the breaking of a holy heart that God in Christ tasted death for every man.

The Tragic Schism : Has it been Healed ?

I

Modern literature has sometimes come within sight of this ultimate problem, usually, alas ! to declare it insoluble. " Yes, I forgive you," a capable author makes one of his characters declare ; " but if I cared for you, forgiveness would be impossible." Forgiveness, that is to say, is a transaction which indifference may find possible : for love it is impossible. But the forgiveness which the cold heart finds easy to offer is no forgiveness. Therefore real forgiveness is impossible.

The same result has been reached from another direction. A few years ago Mr. Bernard Shaw declared that he could not believe in a God who forgave. Nature, and the pitiless law of righteousness which pervades nature, seem utterly unforgiving. Forgiveness, he argued, must be meaningless to a perfect being.

There is an element of moral truth in both points of view. The forgiveness of the easy, genial, mild-mannered man whom we familiarly call " a lump of good nature " is just about as unreal as the forgiveness of cold indifference. But love is not good nature, soft-heartedness. The glory of love lies in the moral fibres of truth, and trust, and loyalty out of which it is woven. Forgiveness cannot come lightly from injured love. Only an expenditure of moral passion, amounting sometimes to heart-break, can heal the broken moral fibres which are the strength of love. God is Love. It must cost Him an infinite agony to forgive.

75

Who was Jesus of Nazareth?

Again, holiness is not cold, impassive justice, it is not an impersonal, pitiless, natural law, it is not a stern and rigid Puritanism of character, harsh, uncompromising, and uncharitable in its judgments of men. It is something more awesome still. It is Conscience : it is Justice throbbing with all the sensitiveness of personality. It is the obverse side of Love. God is Holy Love. And therefore intercourse between the perfectly Pure Being and the soul that has done a repulsive deed can be restored only at a tremendous cost of moral passion.

An illustration will help to give point to the argument. Tennyson, in his " Idylls of the King," makes Prince Arthur come to see his faithless queen in the convent whither she has fled to hide herself. We see the wretched lady grovelling, " with her face against the floor " :

> There with her milk white arms and shadowy hair
> She made her face a darkness from the King:
> And in the darkness heard his armed feet
> Pause by her; then came silence, then a voice,
> Monotonous and hollow like a ghost's
> Denouncing judgment.

On and on goes this cold, sad purity, recounting all the terrible consequences of the sin. And then we hear him say :

> " Lo! I forgive thee, as Eternal God
> Forgives."

But was it forgiveness ? Apart altogether from the fact that the magnanimity is too conscious of itself to have any kinship with the Divine, was the king's deed a genuine forgiveness ? Listen to him further speaking to his queen :

> "I cannot touch thy lips, they are not mine,
> But Lancelot's : nay, they never were the King's.
> I cannot take thy hand ; that too is flesh,
> And in the flesh thou hast sinn'd ; and mine own flesh,
> Here looking down on thine polluted, cries
> ' I loathe thee.' "

Was that forgiveness ? Is that how you conceive " Eternal God forgives " ? Yet, in its very failure we can catch a glimpse of the tragic import of a real forgiveness to Holy Love. All the agony of the offence must be suffered and borne in true forgiveness. And in order that we may have the full problem before us we must again remind ourselves that true repentance is an attempt to see our sin through the eyes of the holy, injured God. Because of the stain and blur of sin that is impossible for the wrong-doer in his own strength alone. The question, therefore, is, Has God accomplished forgiveness ? Has God forgiven us with a forgiveness so wide and so deep that it can take our poor, puny, broken penitence up into itself, and make it perfect for us ? Has God given us such an assurance of forgiveness as contains in it the full and tragic avowal of the agony sin causes in His holy heart, and the unspeakably bitter confession, *for us*, of the infinite heinousness of sin ? The answer is the Crucified Christ.

Who was Jesus of Nazareth?

II

We need not linger long over the false distinction sometimes drawn between the outward event and the moral significance of the event. We have not stated the *fact* until we have stated the spiritual content and implications of the fact. It is not just the wooden Cross on the hill Calvary, and the blood that dropped there from His mortal flesh, that constitutes God's forgiveness. The world has seen thousands of crucifixions. Some were mere malefactor's gibbets—the legal penalty of a crime. Some were the result of a sad mistake—a blind miscarriage of justice, exciting only pity. Some were tragic—a good man misunderstood, the clash of opposing rights, a loving heart impaled to save another. These evoke admiration for the heroism of the sufferer : there is only one Cross in all the world's history that constrains us to adoration and awe. Why ? Because of the Person who was crucified. Not a criminal—it was the criminals who did the deed—but the one perfectly holy and loving Man. In Him all the love and holiness of God flowed out into human life without restriction and without alloy.

It is not merely to the death, but to the moral meaning of the life that ended thus, we have to look. And it is not we alone who, now that it is past, see its significance : it is Christ Himself that *exhibited* its significance to us. The outward facts of the Passion are nothing apart from the significance

The Tragic Schism : Has it been Healed ?

He saw, and felt, and lived out in them ; His dying nothing apart from His willing to die. Through the insight which belongs only to perfect purity and love, He alone in the world of men achieved an unbroken communion with God which shaped itself into the unique experience of Sonship. And He felt and responded to the urge and summons of this experience to bring the God He knew and realised within His own spirit, down into the lives of men. He alone apprehended with every power and faculty of His being the supreme purpose of God in History. He alone could and did surrender His will in all its unblemished freedom and integrity to be the instrument through which the Divine Will could perfectly operate to that end—the end, namely, of lifting a kingdom of souls into perfect communion with God. It was because He deliberately and in utter humility identified His life's work with that Purpose, as His vocation in a sinful world, that the Cross became for Him a moral and at the same time a Divine necessity. And the vicarious shame which laid its ever-deepening burden on His pure soul, the pity and bleeding compassion which filled His heart of love to overflowing, as He faced the misery of mankind, were really and actually at last within the limits of humanity the Agony of the Holy Love of God. This Passion of His was more ; it was the completion of that Agony—the necessary deed in Time, the climax in the forth-flowing energy of the Divine Forgiveness.

79

Who was Jesus of Nazareth?

Gethsemane is therefore the key to the Cross. And it was Christ's response to the call of God in His soul—His deliberate dedication of Himself to the cause of Humanity for His Father's sake—that led inevitably to Gethsemane. And that solemn self-consecration was the first act of His ministry—the submitting to Baptism. *Christ's whole life was the Crucifixion.* Ever and anon there came to Him a thorn, or a nail, or a spear of human sin driven into His quivering, sinless soul. The Cross was scored on the very door by which He entered our humanity—born like a waif, beneath the thatch of an outhouse, beside some cattle beasts. His whole life long He was impaled on the world's hate and shame. Ending at last in one awful hour of horror and darkness, it was simply the unfolding of what the touch of sin means to a being of perfect holiness and love. " In the death of great men the completion of their lives often lies. . . . So it is in a yet deeper sense with the life of Jesus. . . . It was the culmination in a scene in which past, present, and future were gathered into one that was the truth of that life. Not in the mere temporal succession of the events, . . . but in action in which duration in time became of merely secondary importance, existed for (Him) and for us the culminating instant which became eternity."[1]

[1] Haldane, *Pathway to Reality.*

The Tragic Schism : Has it been Healed ?

If we here recall an old controversy, it is only that we may use it to help in the unfolding of our argument. A generation or two ago this was the question that troubled religious thought : Is it merely we who need to be reconciled to God, or does God also need to be reconciled to us ? In the ultra-Calvinistic view, it was God that needed to be reconciled to us. In its extreme form God appears as a kind of Moloch of well-nigh implacable wrath, requiring and demanding the butchery of a sacrifice of pure and spotless innocence, ere His thirst for vengeance can be slaked ; holding His pitiless hand with reluctance from thrusting men down to the fires of hell, and only because His own Son spilt out His blood before Him, to pay down to the uttermost farthing all that His wrath demanded of the helpless sinner. It was this grotesque travesty of " the mystery of Godliness " that George Macdonald preached against in all his books with such fiery and rebellious energy. The old grandmother, in one of his stories, prays to God that her laddie's soul might be saved from the everlasting fire : " O God, I wad burn in hell for him masel', gin ye wad let him aff." It is a touching picture of a heart that is almost Divine staggering blindly under the cruel weight of this iron dogma— that God's heart is an eternal wrath which only an infinite sacrifice will satisfy. God is not visible in the woman's *creed :* God is visible in her blinded heart that would burn to save a soul. The life of religion has often been injured by the abstractions and distinctions of theology. And this is one of the saddest instances—the habit of thinking of God as a far-off, passive, severe, cold Justice; and of Christ as hanging on the Cross enduring the penalty for man's sin, offering a sacrifice to appease Divine Wrath, acting out a tragic spectacle to wring the heart of God into relenting. The one fact we must firmly grasp, and never let go, is that God is in the whole transaction from beginning to end. We might say that there are not three parties concerned in this matter of Divine reconciliation. It is not Christ reconciling another, namely, God, to a third party, man. There are only two parties concerned in the transaction—the holy and loving Father, *God in Christ*, reconciling *us*—to Himself. Altered to agree with that old and cruel view, the Golden Text would run : " God so *hated* the world that the Son had to be killed,"—no ! it is too horrible to go any further. All the Agony of God was there in the Sufferer on the Cross; " God *so loved* the world." It cost God as much to give as it cost Christ to die. Nay, it was God in Christ that tasted death for us.

Swung away to the opposite pole of thought, the mind then asks, where was the need for this transcendent Agony ? If it was only rebellious man that needed to be reconciled to the Eternal Heart of Holy Love, why did God not choose to offer His pardon to men, standing at an infinite distance ? Why did God not simply declare His forgiveness, and leave the rest to man ? It is just here that the view we have offered of the experience of forgiving comes to its own. To say that it is not God who needs to be reconciled to us, but only we who need to be reconciled to God, is to be labouring still within a false distinction. It is no doubt true that God, who is Holy Love, has ever maintained an unchanging attitude of reconciliation and forgiveness towards men. From the beginning of history He has been bending over the sinner, and saying, " Turn ye, turn ye, why will ye die ? " But it was always wounded Love that uttered the cry. This eternal attitude of God's Spirit has ever cost Him infinite pain, agony, sacrifice. The sinner would never turn, would only ignore God's call, if he thought that God was just a great mass of mere good nature, whose one desire was to make everybody comfortable, and who simply doled out His effortless forgiveness, wherever He got the least opportunity, no matter though the Universe were reduced to a perfect chaos, where all trace of the difference between right and wrong was lost. The forgiveness of indifference and of mere good nature is no forgiveness. But surely that is not the reconciliation that exists for ever in idea and in longing in the heart of God. God's forgiveness is the attitude of a heart full of the most poignant and tragic moral perception; of One to whom every thread of the web of life and history, so terribly tangled by sin, is one shuddering mass of living pain ; of One who knows and is ready to experience—blessed be His name! who *has* experienced—the full cost of spiritual Agony which the situation demands, in order that right may be done by it.

The Godhead is neither a mass of indifference, nor a mass of sentiment, nor a mass of cold, pitiless justice. The Divine Heart is Holy Love. He neither ignores sin nor condones it nor sentences it *ab extra*. He *bears* it. He judges men, only by bearing sin. Christ died for the difference between right and wrong. In Him God pronounced final judgment on sin by enduring the last extremity of its agony. Christ took that agony into His pure, kind heart in order that He might say to us, " I am God's forgiveness to you." That is the only forgiveness that will satisfy my sinful heart. The crucified Christ is my assurance of reconciliation ; He is the pledge of the Divine Condescension, the cost of the Divine Forgiveness, the certainty of Love's eternal agony. It is as though God's heart had broken over a lost world, and in that deed of history which culminated on Calvary, the veil were lifted for a little from off the face of the Infinite Sorrow, and sinful men were given a glimpse of this eternal tragedy.

IV

How does it all spell out into reconciliation for each of us ? The passion of repentance and the passion of forgiveness that meet and mingle in the bitter-sweetness of a reconciliation are, it may with truth be said, not two experiences, but one. The more perfect the restoration, the more completely is all the spiritual commotion of pain and joy involved a single experience. Love has been defined as the heart finding itself in another. Repentance is just love finding itself in the reproach that speaks in the heart of the injured friend. Forgiveness is simply love finding itself in all the broken sorrow of the offender. These are not really two experiences but one, in the moment of reconciliation. The symbolical action of embracing is an attempt of flesh and blood to express, what we cannot well express in words, that there are no longer two estranged lives, at such a supreme moment, but that " the two souls like two dew-drops have rushed into one." It is in the unutterable depths of such an experience that there is at-one-ment. Christ is our Symbol in the healing of the tragic schism between the sinful soul and God. He is God's embrace of us. His Cross is the mystic meeting-place of the injured God and the offending human soul. The old word runs : " To err is human, to forgive Divine." We may be allowed to alter it slightly : " To repent is human, to forgive Divine." What we mean is that though repentance and forgiveness are the two sides of the one experience, yet when the matter is between man and God, repentance is only a finite and broken and far-off reflexion of what is experienced in forgiving. Forgiveness is the great Divine reality, in which alone all the agony of the offence is known, which alone contains in all its fulness the true sorrow for sin. Within God's forgiveness there is wrought out for us everything that is lacking in our repentance ; —nay, it is God's forgiveness which, in the first instance, makes us forgivable by making us repentant.

Thus, while Christ's Passion is the Holy God pronouncing judgment on, by bearing, sin, Christ's Passion is at the same time the sorrow of the sinner's confession, the perfect Amen (as Dr. M'Leod Campbell calls it) out of the heart of humanity to the reproach that speaks in God's injured Holy Love. Even so the hot tears of a mother over her wayward child, while they are a symbol of the cost she had to pay in the act of reconciliation, are a pathetic confession also—to her own love, but for her child's sake—of *his* sin. The case is not unknown, indeed, of mothers who, when the call came to them to forgive, actually responded to it with such passion and intensity, that they for the moment fancied it was they who had to *be forgiven !* So completely had their love set them in the room and stead of their child. The case of Pendennis and his mother comes to mind—surely one of the most exquisite instances of reconciliation in secular literature.

" ' Yes, my child, I have wronged you—thank God—I have wronged you ! . . . Come away,

The Tragic Schism : Has it been Healed?

Arthur—not here. I want to ask my child to
forgive me—and—and my God to forgive me;
and to bless you, and love you, my son.' He led
her, tottering, into the room and closed the door.
. . . Ever after, ever after, the tender accents of
that voice faltering sweetly at his ear,—the look of
the sacred eyes, beaming with an affection unutterable—the quiver of the fond lips, smiling mourn-
fully—were remembered by the young man. And
at his best moments, and at his hours of trial and
grief, and at his times of success or well-doing, the
mother's face looked down upon him, and blessed
him with its gaze of pity and purity, as he saw it
in that night when she yet lingered with him; and
when she seemed, ere she quite left him, an angel
transfigured and glorified with love—for which
love, as for the greatest of the bounties and wonders
of God's provision for us, let us kneel and thank
Our Father. . . . He told her the story, the
mistake regarding which had caused her so much
pain. . . . Never again would he wound his
own honour or his mother's pure heart. . . .
But she said it was she who had been proud and
culpable, and she begged her dear boy's pardon.
. . . As they were talking the clock struck nine,
and she reminded him how, when he was a little
boy, she used to go up to his bedroom at that hour
and hear him say, ' Our Father.' And once more,
oh, once more, the young man fell down at his
mother's knees and sobbed out the prayer which the

Divine Tenderness uttered for us, and which has
been echoed for twenty ages since by millions of
sinful and humbled men. And as he spoke the last
words of the supplication, the mother's head fell
down on her boy's, and her arms closed round him,
and together they repeated the words ' for ever
and ever,' and ' Amen.' "

Yes, it is a strangely moving experience, to have
gone to a person to ask pardon for some offence,
and to have felt the unearthly shame and humiliation
of being actually asked for forgiveness by the person
we had wronged. Even in that pathetic illusion of
love's blindness we get a hint of the inner mystery
of the Divine Forgiveness. Such an experience is
shot through with the lights and shadows of Eternity.
It brings us to the foot of the Cross. Not that
God's Spirit in Christ's Passion confesses *our* sin
to *us ;* but that, identifying Himself with humanity
there, and bowing side by side with men within that
transcendent, all-enclosing glory of Truth and
Holiness which is the very ground and condition of
His own Love, and upon which the stability of the
universe depends, He makes (to His own greater
Self, as it were), for us, and with us, the great
reconciling confession. We cannot repent as we
ought to repent, and we know we cannot. But at
Christ's Cross we are assured that God's Forgiveness
contains everything that our poor, broken, and
flickering heart-sorrow lacks. Is there any Sorrow
like unto that Sorrow ? All my penitence, all my

confession, is there—all my defeated hope and inward shame, all my blighted purity and the sense of doom—there in the heart of that agony of the Forgiveness of God. " And the benefit of it we accept, as we accept a mother's prayers and tears, as something our selfishness has required, but which, henceforth, we trust, our selfishness shall never shame."

v

Here, at the end, we find ourselves still standing on the shore of the ocean of the " mystery of Godliness," seeking only to read the message of the music of its falling waves. It *is* a mystery ; but of light, not of darkness. It is simple with love's simplicity : it is exhaustless as love is exhaustless. A child can begin to understand It ; but the eyes of faith go searching out the length and breadth, the heights and depths of it, only to be blinded with excess of light.

Standing afar off the remorseful Peter beheld the Cross ; and he wrote, long after, of " the precious blood of Christ, as of a Lamb without blemish, spotless—predestined even before the foundation of the world." The sight convinced him that the agony which was unveiled there was an agony which slept in the breast of God before the beginning of time. And in the great vision of the consummation of human history, there is seen " in the midst of the Throne . . . a Lamb

. . . slain." That vision is a reflexion of the mind of the beloved disciple who stood beneath the Cross.

Above, behind, and in the Cross of Calvary there is the Eternal Cross, sin's perpetual wound in the holy heart of God. Calvary was the completing, the filling full of the anguish in the experience of God forgiving. But the moaning undertone of the Divine Pain stretches through all the span of time, and out beyond it, both before and after. The dull ears of the human race, confused with the wandering sounds of earth, have seldom heard it. Once or twice has an echo been caught by some earnest, listening soul, and written by the Spirit of God upon the sacred page. The impulse which prompted the immortal picture of the Suffering Servant was surely a heaving of the anguished breast of God. Then with the coming of Christ, and through the few short rushing years of the Saviour's ministry, " swift up the sharp scale of sobs God's breast did lift," till it ended in the mighty, yearning sigh which broke upon the earth and made the Cross.

V

The Conversion of Peter

PRINCIPAL LINDSAY, the historian of the Reformation, used to say that the Christian Church had lived by revivals. With one important addition that might be considered the law of life for Christianity. The history of the Church is in a very real sense the history of its great revivals *and its great conversions.* How much Christianity owes, for example, to the conversion of Chalmers, of Wesley, of Bunyan, of Luther, of St. Francis of Assisi, of St. Augustine, of St. Paul. We wish to claim here that the Christian Church began its career in a conversion—the commotion which overtook the soul of Peter after his denial. This was not the first time Peter was converted : there are some people built that way. By the shore of the Lake of Galilee he had experienced something like a change of heart when he cried, " Depart from me for I am a sinful man, O Lord." But this which happened after his denial was undoubtedly the most significant of these upheavals in his soul. It was the laying of the foundation stone, the rock on which the Master built His Church.

There is nothing rock-like about the character of Peter as we find it in the Gospel pages ; a big, impulsive, blustering fellow, a natural leader among the fishermen of the Lake, fond not merely of airing his opinions, but of thrusting them upon you ; and yet inconstant as spring winds, blowing hot and blowing cold, loud as a gale and timid as an evening breeze, violent but fitful. One day, among his comrades of the oar, passing sceptical remarks about the new Reformer, and the next day, prostrate on the shore at His feet, crying, " Depart from me . . . "—crying " Depart," though it was the very last thing he wanted Him to do. Again, one morning, soaring in ecstatic speech (" Thou art the Christ, the Son of the living God "), and in the evening, letting the devil get the better of him (" Far be it from Thee, Lord ; this shall never be to Thee "). One moment, contrary (" Thou shalt never wash my feet "), and the next moment, utterly consenting (" Lord, not my feet only, but also my hands and my head "). Rash in fight (" One of them "—John says it was Peter—" drew a sword and smote the High Priest's servant's ear "), and equally headlong in flight (" They *all* forsook Him and fled "). Swearing eternal loyalty in the deep night, swearing his denial before the next day's dawn, then weeping his repentance when the cock was crowing to the breaking skies.

This last scene was where the great upheaval began.

And if, humanly speaking, the fate, nay, the existence, of the Christian Church hung on this man's experience, how can the heart of Christendom fail to be drawn towards it ? Unprecedented this miracle of conversion may have been, perhaps even, in some of its features, never to be repeated. Yet it is the type and symbol and key to the story of all who have turned to the Lord Jesus since Peter's day. "When thou art converted," the words run in the Gospel story ; and whether you believe, with us, that Jesus spoke the words, or whether you think they are a reflection of the memory of the early Christian Church, there is no shadow resting on the fact they proclaim : the words would not have been written had they not come true. On its Divine side it was a vision of the risen Christ at last, but on its human side, as these words testify, it was a real and genuine conversion. It is the human side that concerns us mainly here.

I

Picture him, first, if you can, in Caiaphas' judgment hall. Under the porticoes close at hand the travesty of a trial is still in progress. There is the Accused, His arms lashed to His sides with thongs, His face still pale with the wrestling in the Garden. And here in the centre of the courtyard His disciple sits, in the flickering light of the brazier fire, dazed amid the ribald soldiers and the jesting menials—sits, and broods, and warms his hands. It was an ugly dream—this, he was living through. Yonder, where the torches blazed on the glittering robes of the Sanhedrin, was the false grandeur of

Who was Jesus of Nazareth?

Israel's faded glory. And yet how terribly real it seemed to the disciple's eyes that night! All things else were fading for him, drifting down the wind: the thronging crowds in Galilee that hung on those lips so silent now; the power of Jesus' words to quell the demons; the happy stories that He used to tell; the long, still nights of sacred friendship, lived, as it seemed, close up beside the gates of heaven; the love that welled from His heart; the pity and purity that glowed in His eyes—fading, fading. And with these things the certainty of the heavenly Father's care—all that the Master had made them so sure of concerning God—fading out, as it seemed, beyond recall. In its stead, the picture of the old Jewish God, which the synagogue teachers had taught him in his boyhood, rose up once more in Peter's mind. His confused, bewildered brain began to play tricks with his vision. The tribunal over yonder blurred for a moment. The hollow majesty of the court of the Sanhedrin gave way before a far more awful vision. He now saw the Lord God Almighty sit in the High Priest's chair. He heard a great voice, stern and dreadful, utter the accusations against the Master. It was the voice of the relentless course of events that had pursued the Nazarene and brought him to this hour. Was not the voice of history the voice of God? Over those three swift years the finger of Fate was writing " Failure." The law of righteousness which runs through life was pronouncing judgment. It was all a pitiful and tragic mistake.

The Conversion of Peter

God was vindicating Himself in this terrible dispensation of Providence. At the best, the Man of Nazareth was utterly self-deceived. At the worst, He was—a rank Deceiver! Peter shivered and stretched his hands still nearer to the fire. The blood in his veins ran cold. . . . And then a face peered close to Peter's through the flickering firelight; a taunting finger pointed and a girl-slave's voice cried, " This man also was with Jesus of Nazareth." In an instant the fatal denial slipped from Peter's lips; then, stung by the repeated taunt, it rose to a torrent of oaths and curses.

II

But see! the mock trial is over. The Sanhedrin is rising. The Prisoner is being led away across the courtyard. The craven disciple lifts his eyes a moment. And the Lord turns and looks on Peter —a long, sad, earnest gaze of wounded love—the haunting look of one marked out for death. No word is spoken. The disciple's eyes are rivetted a moment in fear and shame. Then the face is slowly turned away; and the retreating form vanishes through the gateway. The night hid Him. " And—Peter— remembered." Painfully he struggled to his feet. He staggered out of the courtyard. And in the pallor of the grey dawn, his heart broke; he gave way to bitter weeping.

What was the flood of memory that rushed upon his soul? He had seen his Master standing there, as he tells us long after—sinless, without a blemish, without a stain, without a word of guile in His mouth; reviled, and yet reviling not; tortured—without a breath of imprecation from His lips; putting to silence the ignorance of foolish men. The majesty of it rose up before him overwhelmingly now. And with it his memory flew away out yonder where the pale light was breaking in the northern skies. All the past came flooding swiftly back: the great words, the great deeds, the great nights of fellowship with Jesus, the self-forgetting pity and compassion, the pure love, the pure life, the unutterable sincerity, the transparency of soul—it had all shone on him once more through those eyes that turned and looked on him in Caiaphas' judgment hall. He deceived! He an impostor! "No, no, no!" a voice in Peter's heart began to cry, "let all things else be false, but He was true. Chaos and darkness round me, but there my Master stands, the one luminous and radiant certainty for me. Oh, the disloyalty that could deny that soul of truth! Blind heart, deceitful above all things and desperately wicked! Speaking evil of the things I understood not! I am no more worthy to be called a disciple."

So, through that fateful dawning, when the Master passed, and turned, and looked, and spoke no word, this stricken and repentant heart lay weeping in the dust. And then he rose. One fixed resolve possessed him. Somehow to snatch a moment at the Master's feet, and plead for forgiveness, cost him what it may. Better to die forgiven than to live cast out.

III

See him hastening now along the street to Pilate's tribunal! And listen! A cry breaks on his ears. The roar of the rabble. What are those mad voices saying ? " Away with Him! Crucify! Crucify! " Peter is too late. Hot, dishevelled, desperate, he quickens his pace. At length he catches sight of the ghastly procession melting through the city gate. He follows running. Stunned and dazed with horror, he pauses in the shadow of the city walls beyond the gate ; and there he watches the gruesome gibbets being reared upon the hill. A witness of the Passion so he tells us in his letter afterwards.

Little by little he draws nearer to the hill. He witnesses the dying thief redeemed and promised bliss with Christ in Paradise. In Paradise ? What confidence, what certitude! Out of the starkest and most sordid death, He speaks of passing hence to Paradise. And

> Did ever paladin, adventuring out
> Upon the great uncharted enterprise,
> Choose for companion in the crucial bout
> A sorrier squire with whom to agonise ?

A convicted thief! Surely there is hope for Peter still. Is it yet too late for him to kneel and plead for one releasing word ? Hearken! " My God, my God, why hast Thou forsaken me ? " The parched lips are moistened. Then, " Father, into Thy hands I commend My spirit." His head droops. He is dead.

A horror of great darkness rushes over Peter's soul. Hateful the hissing crowd! Hateful the green hill, and the dusty road, and the black sky! Nothing pure and holy in all that landscape but the Figure on the Cross! Nothing true in all the universe but Him! Last night Peter denied Him because God seemed to be proving His life was mistaken and vain. But to-day Peter has faith in nothing else but Him ; and yonder He dies like a felon. Is there a God in heaven that can look upon that Cross and vindicate His own righteousness ? Nay, God has erred, God is powerless, God is a demon, there is no God !

IV

Eleven men are huddled in a darkened room behind closed doors. See, there is our man somewhat apart from the rest, his face haggard, his brow clouded, his eyes agleam with something kin to madness. For a new thought has entered Peter's mind. From denial of Christ in the name of God, he had swung to denial of God in the name of Christ. But those cries from the Cross had brought more memories thronging thick and fast. Jesus had not denied God even on the Cross. God-forsaken, as it seemed, He had called Him " My God " still. With His latest breath He had committed His spirit into His Father's hands. If Jesus was true, then the great fact for which Jesus lived must be true. Nay, the great fact on which He had staked His life could not possibly be false. God was no demon, but the Heavenly Father. There was nothing that Jesus was more certain of than that. It was through His consciousness of God—we take the thought again from Peter's letter—that Jesus endured grief, suffering wrongfully. All through His life the Father was as real and certain to Jesus as the sunlight ; and to the bitter end—in spite of the black hounds of Fate that had driven Him to the agony of the garden and the shame of the Cross—to the bitter end, Jesus was entirely satisfied with God. If Peter truly believed in Jesus, he dared not deny Jesus' God. These were the two certainties that remained with Peter now from his fellowship with Jesus—the memory of the pure and perfect life that lately lived with them, and the thought of the Father God in heaven. But the Cross, the inexorable Cross that stood between— what could it mean in a world where God reigned ?

Have we ever drawn towards the Cross from that angle ? The world has been trying to put it out of count to-day. It has been trying to work out a religion of Jesus without reckoning on the Cross. It is content to leave it there as a mysterious surd in God's universe—no power of God unto salvation, only an inexplicable problem. And what has been the result ? The result has ever been just what we have been trying to trace in Peter's experience.

God, Jesus and the Cross. And so long as the Cross has not been taken into the reckoning, no meaning found for it in God's plan, either Jesus has been counted a mistaken enthusiast, broken on the world's wheel, or God is dethroned—conceived of, as Mr. H. G. Wells has conceived of Him—as a struggling God, blundering along with a universe that has got completely out of hand. We call you back to the mind of Jesus to-day. Whatever else is sure in history, this is sure : the world has no holier fact than the fact of Christ, the Alone Pure. And Jesus knew no more certain fact than the reality of the All-Great and the All-Loving Heavenly Father. Blessed be His pure heart, for He saw God, and made us sure of Him. Bring the Cross into the light of those two great certainties, and you *cannot get away from it* until you have found a place for it in God's plan.

v

How did it fare with Peter and his problem ? We may be very sure of this, that he did see light at last. Men have turned reproachful eyes on Paul for hiding Christ's message of the Kingdom behind the terrible beam on which He died. The fact is, it was Peter who first saw the Cross and its solemn meaning. And it was the great certainties of Christ's life, and God's Fatherhood which Christ revealed—those certainties confronting his own lost, hopeless, bankrupt and disloyal soul—that drove him to seek and seek until he found. Where it was the light came, we shall never know. But on some Emmaus road, on those first days of his distraction, his heart began to burn within him. And once again it was memory that set his sad mind moving, as he broke bread in remembrance of Him, perhaps. Ah, Paul may be the apostle of Faith, and John the apostle of Love, but Peter is the apostle of Memory. Long ago, in Peter's noblest hour at Cæsarea Philippi, did not the Master begin to tell them He must die ? Over and over again He told them on that solemn passion journey to Jerusalem from the Mount of Transfiguration. Beginning with Moses and the prophets, echoes of the ancient scriptures on which Jesus leaned came back to him. The Suffering Servant " must die " ; it was the Divine necessity, the Divine Plan. The Cross was God's chosen way for Jesus, Love's only choice in a world of sin.

How do we know that Peter found it so ? Listen to him on the streets of Jerusalem seven weeks after Calvary : " Jesus of Nazareth, a man approved of God . . . was delivered by the determinate counsel and foreknowledge of God. . . . And God hath made this same Jesus, whom ye have crucified, both Lord and Christ. . . . Repent and be baptised, every one of you, in His name for the remission of sins. . . . He is the Prince of Life, . . . and those things which God hath showed by the mouth of all His prophets, that Christ should suffer, He hath so fulfilled." Listen to him before the Sanhedrin : " There is none other name under heaven given among men whereby we must be saved." Listen to him when he writes from Rome long after to Asiatic converts : " Christ also hath once suffered for sins, the just for the unjust, that He might bring us to God." And this other amazing word : " Ye are redeemed . . . with the precious blood of Christ, . . . a Lamb without blemish . . . foreordained before the foundation of the world."

Yes, it was the sight of that terrible Cross on the hill, seen by the remorseful Peter standing afar, that came back to him in after days, and convinced him that the agony that was unveiled there was an agony that lay hidden in the bosom of God from all eternity. That was the meaning of the Cross. It was the unveiling of the agony of the forgiving God. Christ is the cost of God's forgiveness. And God is still on the throne of the universe, but His throne is a Cross, ever and only a Cross. That was the discovery that brought the disloyal Peter back to God. That is the discovery that still avails to bring the sin-stricken heart to God.

VI

But there was more to follow. This was not the end ; in a sense it was only the beginning of Peter's experience. Step by step, as he recalled the past, his soul had been climbing from the pit of his despair. For with the memory of the death foretold, came the memory also of Jesus' prediction of victory, His rising from the grave. Yes, if it was God's plan for Jesus that He should die for human sin, it must be part of that same plan that He should conquer death that Peter might live. *He*, the perfect soul, the Pioneer of Life—lost forever in the night of death ? Perish the impious thought ! " It was not possible that *He* should be holden of death." This disciple who had proved so false to his Lord must die of grief if that grim Cross remained relentlessly between. But Peter lived. And why ? Because his Master was alive. The deep peace passing all understanding, the peace of forgiveness that was falling round his soul, was the living Spirit of his Master, taking possession of him, laying His hand on him in benediction, as of old beside the lake. And His voice, the old familiar voice, was whispering in his soul. Then somehow his eyes were opened, and he saw the Lord. Heart melted over into heart and they were one for evermore. And Peter's companions caught the contagion, were lifted into Peter's ecstasy, as they listened to his broken words of joy. Before their vision also, the presence of the risen Christ became actualised. So the converted Peter strengthened his brethren.

The Resurrection experience ! Why has it never been vouchsafed to us in just the way the disciples witnessed it ? *Has* it never been repeated ? The Sadhu Sundar Singh says he saw Him. Other saints have said the same. We have invented all sorts of reasons to explain the non-repetition of the resurrection experience. The truth is, we fail to realise the presence of our Risen Lord just in proportion as our hearts are unprepared and unfitted for the experience. If we had passed through the deeps of Peter's experience, we would have realised the sacred presence as completely as he. We *have* felt it in proportion to our fitness. He is alive. And He is here. And the Church will see Him and know Him again, when it makes a whole-hearted return to the Cross. " Blessed be God," said Peter ; he had hardly put pen to paper to write that letter of his when he was constrained to write the words, " Blessed be the God and Father of our Lord Jesus Christ, Who according to His abundant mercy has begotten us again to a living hope by the resurrection of Jesus Christ from the dead." The Cross standing up into the light of the resurrection, that is the saving discovery. " He hath given us rest by His sorrow, and life by His death."

The Mind of the Master on Immortality

VOICES from the dawn of History—the pyramids and the Egyptian Book of the Dead (among the oldest extant creations of man) ; voices from beyond that dawn—the superstitions of earth's most backward tribes, or the tumuli that beckon to us with their grey, pathetic stone fingers from many a green hillside in our native land, all alike bear testimony to the age-long preoccupation of the human mind with the Great Misgiving : " If a man die, shall he live again ? " The sombre question strikes on the heart like an icy breath of East wind wafted through the summer's glory—like the shadow when a swift cloud obscures the sun. The question haunts the earth with cold and cruel persistence.

Yet these same ancient relics bear an equally decisive witness to the everlasting " Yea," with which the constant and almost universal human hope has made answer to the Great Fear. What response has the Lord and Master of human life to make to this ancient and holiest hope of man ?

I

At first sight it strikes one as remarkable that in the first three Gospels, where we come nearest to His authentic, living words, only one occasion is reported, on which Jesus unburdens His heart in direct and specific terms upon this subject. It touches us to remember that it was close up under the shadow of the swiftly coming Cross. In the courts of the great Temple, on one of the closing Passion days, some Sadducees, men who held there was no rising from the dead, propounded an extreme instance of the working of the Levirate law : seven brothers married in turn to the same woman, all dying childless. Whose wife would she be in the Resurrection ?

Jesus said to them : " Is not this where you go wrong ? You understand neither the Scriptures nor the power of God. When they rise from the dead, there is no marrying or being married ; they are as the angels are in heaven. But as to the dead, and the fact that they rise to life, have you never read in the book of Moses at the passage about the bush, how God said to him : ' I AM THE GOD OF ABRAHAM AND THE GOD OF ISAAC AND THE GOD OF JACOB ' ? He is not the God of dead men, but of living people ! You are far astray ! "

To the casual and inattentive reader it is at first sight a disconcerting reply. " Is the whole case for personal survival beyond death based upon a verbal quibble ? " To answer that cry of pained disappointment, it is unnecessary to shelter oneself behind the suggestion that Peter (for it is probably to him that we owe the reminiscence) only repeated in the hearing of Mark a fragment of Jesus' reply

The Mind of the Master on Immortality

that clung imperfectly to his memory, though doubtless that is quite true. For in reality the reply as we have it goes deep into the heart of the holiest human experience.

We feel quite sure of that. And yet to us the most precious thing about the reply lies, not in the spoken word, but in the manner, the mood, the temper in which it was spoken. Nearly all our New Testament translators have failed to reproduce the emphasis, nay, the vehemence, the throbbing passion that fired the whole being of our Lord as He spoke these words. The emotion rises in a swift crescendo from the first syllable of His reply to its close. The assurance, the authority that speak in the opening question, the amazement at His challengers, the unhesitating conviction that their whole outlook was wrong, ends in the holy indignation that thrills through the final phrase : πολὺ πλανᾶσθε—you are far astray !

Much that Jesus said has been lost forever to mankind. But one feels that this word could not have been lost. The Divine Spirit has seen to it that the memories of those who listened should not fail us here. For in this word thus recorded by the finger of God upon the sacred page, our Lord has flung Himself into the lists, standing between His lady, His bride elect, the company of the faithful, and those spiritual vandals with their sceptic spears. With one clean sword stroke He has cleft through the clever intellectual trifling which dared to lay impious hands upon the ark of man's most sacred longings and desires. πολὺ πλανᾶσθε ! With that word Jesus constituted Himself forever the guardian of the eternal human hope.

And what does this amazed anger that informs His words imply ? Have you ever tried to listen to the strains of some great symphony stealing through the quiet moonlight and experienced the annoyance, the irritation, the almost intolerable distraction caused by the barking of some miserable dog ? Have you ever stood to gaze at some fair landscape scene backed by the sublimity of the everlasting hills, the virgin snows of far-off mountain peaks, and been compelled by close proximity, to listen to the idle chatter of a holiday crowd about lost luggage, and the latest scandal, and hotel menu cards, and the stale old puns and jokes of travel ? Your feelings at such a moment were a far-off reflection of the emotion that finds expression in the words of Jesus. Here was one whose whole life was a reverent listening to the immortal harmonies of heaven, one who perpetually gazed upon the land of far distances, annoyed (if one might reverently use the word) because His attention had been withdrawn for a moment from His constant dwelling in the eternities and immensities, to listen to the petty, would-be-superior, logical juggling of men who fancied they could reduce the eternal hope to an absurdity by a few clever but quite irrelevant questions, of men who had first of all rendered themselves incapable of conceiving the true nature of the life everlasting, and then imagined they were attacking and destroying the belief by setting up a bogey of their own creating in order that they might fell it—to their own immense satisfaction. They could not conceive of any possible resurrection life save one which was a sorry repetition of this fading, finite existence, with its tangled human relationships, its limited capacities, its mutually exclusive proprietorships, its mean joys, its pathetic brokennesses, harsh discords, losses, sorrows and despairs.

" And *you* think," He says to them, " to gauge the life everlasting with your small earthly proprieties and conventions ! You think to laugh it out of human thought by depicting it as a place where the complications of earth would be accentuated and brought to a climax in a hopelessly ravelled skein ? The resurrection life ! You simply have not the faintest conception what it means. No wonder you disbelieve in it, if that is all you can make of it. Because you have left God out of account in this life, you have thought to thrust the great power of God aside as an irrelevance in the question of the possibility of a life to come ; and you have thought to pooh-pooh men out of their—to you—unmeaning but strangely persistent faith, by building a nightmare out of your materialistic reasonings, and lifting it up in derision, as a description, forsooth, of all that the holiest dreams of humanity amount to ! You are far astray ! "

Who was Jesus of Nazareth ?

Yes, it is only when we feel the amazed anger of Christ upon the only recorded occasion when He was challenged to deal directly with the question of immortality, that we are in a position to evaluate aright the strength of His reply. We are compelled to set the answer of the moment back into the context of the answer which His whole life makes to the Great Misgiving. We are driven back to perceive that the assurance of immortality underlies every word He spoke, every thought and emotion of His heart, every prayer He breathed, every decision He made, every deed He wrought among men, and most of all the Cross on which He willed to die. It is one of the fundamental presuppositions of His world-view: it pervades the revelation He has bequeathed to us, as the sunlight does the limpid water of the running stream. It can no more be dissociated from it than heat from fire. It is the splendour of the eastward fronting window in the temple of His mind.

For it is Christ who has made the fact of the presence of God in human life—God's intimate love and care for the human soul—an assured possession of the experience of mankind forever. It is Christ, supremely, who has lifted up human individuality into the light of that presence, and made its immortal worth, its spiritual uniqueness shine out in such a way that all the philosophies—Pantheisms, Pessimisms, Scepticisms, Agnosticisms, which have been offered to the world since then—have inevitably shattered themselves against the rock of this ineradicable conviction. Ever and again the world's thinkers have been compelled to rebuild their systems nearer to the demands of this Divinely re-enforced instinct which they cannot kill.

Let us glance then for a moment at the Master's world-view. We can do so only in broad and general outline. It may truly be said that Jesus was the preacher of a single theme—the Kingdom or the Realm of God. It was the constant subject of His earliest preaching in the sunny days in Galilee : "Repent, for the Realm of God is drawn nigh." The Sermon on the Mount may be called the charter of the Realm. The great majority of the parables are parables of the Realm. His task, as He conceived it, was to establish the Realm and Reign of God on earth, to open the Kingdom of heaven to all believers by His sacrificial life, nay—for it was necessary—by His death upon the Cross. What is the bearing of this great conception which dominated and possessed the mind of Jesus, on the hopes of earth regarding the life everlasting ?

Now the natural human heart is prone to clutch at the most concrete and material picture of what the Kingdom means. "Jesus proclaimed the reality of the Realm of *heaven*," we say. "Oh, then, in His opinion there is a heaven, there is a realm of spiritual life that transcends this life, beyond this world there is a world to come. It is an age that begins when this life ends ; it is a place beyond the clouds and beyond the tomb. And we can believe in the life immortal because Jesus confidently affirmed to all his faithful followers that they would enter and belong to the Kingdom." But we are not here to buttress the instincts of the human heart by an appeal to a vague unexamined phrase. *Was* that what Jesus really meant by the Kingdom ? Was He just a Dreamer, carried away by the beauty of His own dream, as He pictured a sphere of glory in the far-off presence of His Father, where the redeemed entered into unending bliss beyond the grave, a world which was to draw near and be manifested on this earth some day—a great day of blinding light, of resurrection and of judgment ? Was He just another religious enthusiast sharing the Apocalyptic hopes of the fanatics of His people's faith ? And if, to Him also, this kingdom was a mere dream, something of which in His limited, earthly life He had, and could have, no actual experience, what guarantee is it of our eternal hope to hear it repeated and repeated on His lips ? Even in Him may it not be a delusion, a phantasy, a beautiful but pathetic figment of the mind ?

The great battle of New Testament criticism joins its hottest front around this question to-day. The extremists have asserted with their usual confidence, after prodigious microscopical research in the Gospels, that this, or something very like it, was what Jesus really conceived the Kingdom to be.

And scholars have been driven to examine His words again. They have analysed and dissected them. And the result they offer is a bewildering set of contradictions and paradoxes which so vex and pain the seeking soul that he has no heart nor power, either to unite them into one consistent picture, or to choose between them, if they will not coalesce. Sometimes Jesus seems to have thought of the Realm of God as having to do entirely with this life, sometimes as belonging wholly to a life in the unseen. Sometimes He seems to have thought of it as an inward spiritual thing, present now in human life, and capable of being experienced and enjoyed now by the soul; sometimes as an outward something that is yet to be realised some day upon this earth, but in a distant age of the world's history. Sometimes He spoke of it as a thing of slow and gradual growth, coming unobtrusively, imperceptibly among mankind; sometimes again as something supernatural, something that was to descend in spectacular grandeur from the clouds of heaven, and to come suddenly—and soon—upon the earth, like the lightning flashing from end to end of the sky.

And when we try to grasp Jesus' conception of the Kingdom, thus broken by the pedants into these perplexing logical paradoxes, it becomes to us a thing emptied of life and joy. It is as if we had asked the botanist to tell us the wonder and the meaning of the rose; and he were to lay the flower under his merciless dissecting needles, hack it and cut it into petal and sepal, pistil and stamen and ovary; and show us the cells and the vascular bundles, the chlorophyl and protoplasm. We gather the dead fragments together and hide them from our sight. We cannot bear to look on them. That is not the fair, white, lovely thing that woke our wonder. Wistfully we turn away.

We approach another set of experts to ask if they can give us anything more real and satisfying. And we find them waiting for us—a set of teachers who have gone to the opposite extreme from that of the Apocalyptic Theorists. And they bring the Kingdom down to earth out of the clouds with such thoroughness and persistence that they too have succeeded in wearying and nauseating the soul, sick for eternal certainties. They profess to describe what Jesus meant by the Kingdom in a series of long-drawn social programmes, schemes of reform, principles and laws of ethical conduct and political activity; until we get lost, bewildered, out of temper sometimes in the welter. And the soul, the insatiate soul, craving still for eternity, begins to cry out, " Give me bread, bread, not a stone ! "

There is some truth, much truth, in their reasonings, no doubt. But if all that Jesus came to offer us was a programme of social and moral reform for this earth, then it has no answer to make to the Great Misgiving. And if, on the other hand, all that He had to offer us was a dream in the clouds, something beyond His actual experience, offspring of His own untested enthusiasm and imagination, for Him too nothing but a lovely hope, then there is no assurance, no certainty, no solid foothold here for the great human yearning for immortality.

III

What then ?   Shall we not submit to be led once more by Jesus, the poet, the seer, the mystic, but more than all these, the Man of flawless moral insight, up to the heights of His spiritual vision, where we can feel something of the rapture and the glow of the great Reality that possessed Him ; and entering in by the gateway of humility, find it was no dream but a fact, a great moral and spiritual fact, the sure and certain experience of His soul ?   One cannot hope, in a few prosaic sentences, to delineate His experience.   But this much we would dare to say.   The Realm of Heaven, as Jesus saw it, is but the unique and supreme expression of an experience which is the birthright of all mankind.   We are creatures of two worlds, we mortals.   We belong to the outer world of sense, but we have the right of entrance also to an inner world of spirit—of ethical and intellectual values.   And the Realm of Heaven belongs to that inner world, rather, we should say, is that spiritual world, as seen when we have climbed up out of the lowlier and more shaded ways and viewed it from a mountain top of rapture.   The Realm for Jesus, as for us also, is that serene region of thought and hope, of conscience and imagination, into which almost every human soul soars at times in those ecstatic moments which are gifts to us from the infinite mercy of God. God made us for the vision. If we have not reached it of ourselves, God has surely, once at least, drawn near to us in the touch of other lives upon ours—in a child's innocence and clinging love, in a woman's tears, in a friend's devotion, in a hero's sacrifice, in the martyr's contempt of pain and wrong and death, in the saint's passionate yearning for the Face of God, surely at least in our Redeemer's Cross. And in the thrill of recognition of the infinite worth and splendour of such holy facts, the scales have fallen from our eyes, and we have seen the sun-break upon the stainless peaks—we have entered the Kingdom.

Granted that for most of us it is a dim and broken vision, granted that even the divinely gifted poet Dante can only stammer with the mystics when he tries to describe the celestial white rose of Love Divine, and that St. Augustine must needs join company with the poets when he speaks in rhapsody of the City of God, while all alike fall short of the abiding vision of Christ—still it is the same Kingdom seen in varying fullness by us as by Him. It is the birthright of humanity. It is, as has been finely said, " the higher world of white ideals, of broad spiritual expanses, of clean thought and generous service, of just and steadfast vision, of the loving fear of God and the reverent love of men—the world which all men behold sometimes when the clouds break, of which some high souls are the constant citizens, though most of us know it only in the rare hours when almost we are what we would hope to be. This heavenly state, this home of our ideals, is the source of all our light. In it are treasured the perfect types of all good things which can be known by any man, or embodied in any society or in any Church or in any Age of Gold. No faith, no race has any exclusive right to it: it has always been the motherland of all the faithful. What matters the name by which we call it—the New Jerusalem, the Realm of God, Eternal life? What matter whether we speak of it in the language of vision as the Heavenly Zion coming down from on high, or in the language of Ethics as the Chief Good? It is the same whatever it be called, however it be conceived, in whatsoever terms it be described. It is always in heaven yet always on earth, ever present yet ever to be."[1]

But the seeking soul here begins to lose the old familiar foothold once again. Is this really the Kingdom of God as Jesus conceived it? True, this was a real experience in the soul of Jesus. He dwelt constantly in rapturous intercourse with life's sublime ideal. But is the Kingdom of Heaven nothing more than this inner realm of the mind and conscience? Had it no existence apart from His soul? Was it not something less private, more assured, than that? Is there then no heaven, no world to come—no world that is more than simply that spiritual world of soaring ideals, and holy thoughts, and fair

[1] J. H. Leckie, D.D. The World to come and Final Destiny.

memories of friendship and love, which springs into life sometimes in the human soul at its best, and which lived always in the mind of Jesus ?

Here is our answer to that. You do grant that this inner, ideal world was a real and present experience of Jesus ? We might ask, Is there no difference between vision born of fantasy and vision born of moral conviction ? But we do not stay to argue for the ultimate reality of moral and spiritual values. We hasten to place beneath it all the other great, sure fact in the experience of Jesus—namely the presence of God. It is the most wonderful thing in the spiritual history of mankind—Jesus' clear, intimate and abiding sense of the presence of God. It is one of the foundation pillars of the Life unveiled in the Gospels. It cannot be eliminated, or explained away, unless the Gospels themselves can be dissipated into myth and moonshine. And the attempt to do that leads to a historical *reductio ad absurdum.* And it is this realisation of God by Jesus that makes all the difference for this question of human immortality. For—here is the important point for our present purpose—Jesus did not call this inner spiritual world of which we have been speaking the Kingdom of the ideal; He called it the Kingdom—the realm—of *God.* Without this unassailable fact—Jesus' consciousness of, His acquaintanceship, constant fellowship and communion with, God, so close and intimate that He could call Him by no other name than Father—even this ideal

The Mind of the Master on Immortality

Kingdom of the mind might be held to be nothing more than another insubstantial dream, however holy. And its existence in the soul, while it might create the presumption, could not guarantee the truth of the immortality of the soul to which it owed its being. Dreamer and dream might perish together in death.

But the presence of God, the Oversoul, realised in the life of such a soul, makes all the difference between the little candle-flame of hope, blowing in the wind in a dense, dark night, and the full-orbed radiance of daylight certitude. For think what it means. It means His waking to the fact that this inner land of holy vision, this realm of life's white Ideal, *is all realised in the great mind of God*—is in fact the rich fulness of the life and being of the Divine Mind. For when Jesus became alive to the authentic drawing near of God, all this inner world of the Ideal Good, this Kingdom of the mind, became rapidly transformed in every feature of it as by a subtle and powerful alchemy. Those soaring thoughts, insights, aspirations began as it were to lay aside their familiar garb of earth. They became vocal—became filled with the throbbing life of Infinite Personality graciously stooping to whisper its holiest secrets to His soul. God, the Father signed and sealed all Jesus' conjecturings, intuitions, visions of world-truth with His own Divine imprimatur. What may once have seemed His own discoveries in the world of thought, revealed their hidden features now as *disclosures vouchsafed and given* to Him by God His Father. The decisions of His own pure will, made under the light of the Ideal Good, turned out to be inspirations, *corroborations, reinforcements* from the Eternal Will. Every choice of ways in hours of crisis now revealed itself as Divine *leading*. In every labour of love for men He recognised He was being *directed, used*—in His own great word—" *sent*." The Kingdom of the Ideal Good became to Him, in short, the secrets of the Divine Intercourse, the Realm of God, the last Reality. He no longer felt or said " all things have been sought out, discovered by Me "; but "all things have been delivered unto Me by My Father." His spirit knelt in deep humility, while with uplifted eyes He saw the whole starry plan of God unveiled before Him. And in hushed reverence and gratitude He acknowledged His Sonship : " I thank Thee, O Father, LORD of heaven and earth, that Thou hast hid these things from the wise and prudent, and hast revealed them unto babes. Even so, Father, for so it seemed good in Thy sight."

IV

This certainly was what the Kingdom meant for Jesus. That was why He called it the " Realm of God." And we can say at once that if into the life of this One Soul on earth there came this absolutely assured contact with God, a spiritual fact so overwhelming that all who look at it with candid, earnest eyes are compelled to acknowledge it—*that*, of itself, would suffice to establish the abiding reality of the Kingdom of the Ideal, which is the birthright of all men. But we are not called on to rest content with that. Once again we dare to say that, not only this Kingdom of the Ideal, but this consciousness of the presence of God which Jesus possessed, is something from which no soul on earth need wholly be debarred. This too is man's birthright—though forfeited by sin. In all the most sacred records of man's trafficking with the Unseen, as Jesus Himself acknowledged, there is abundant witness to the presence of God having been truly realised again and again in the life of the human soul. And it is this that guarantees the abiding reality of the inner kingdom of the mind. It is rooted and grounded in the life of God. Thus when we soar into this serene region of the soul's inner world we have actually begun in our imperfect, finite way to think God's thoughts after Him; we have become with Him for the moment "spectators of all time and of all existence;" we are partakers in the Divine Life which is the ultimate Reality, sharers already in the Life Eternal.

Once the presence of God has been made sure to us, therefore—and it is the one fact which must come home to us, by the gift of God's own Grace, before we can truly be said to have entered into the Kingdom of God—then the great hope of the human heart has secured a foothold on a rock which cannot be shaken. Man is born to soar and dream, to pant for the infinite, for more life and fuller. The Realm of God is the Divine answer to this divinely planted longing. It is the land where all our holiest dreams come true, nay, where they are already realised and held secure—in the life of God. Man is always waiting till his ship comes home. The Realm of God is the haven where the ship of the soul does at last come home. Heaven is the Presence of God in all His fullness. Immortality, eternal life, is the soul entering at last to dwell forever in God. " Thy heart, dear God, is home to me." Does the soul crave any more heaven than that ? Call heaven a state or a place as you will—it matters not. It has all the reality that the soul craves for when it thinks of heaven as a place, a land, a world. Because we are finite, we must use the earthly features of the life we know to express this aspect of it—we can do no other. Jesus used them too. And they carry in the heart of them the light of self-shining truth, as all poetry does. But heaven has also all the fullness and rich-ness of the soul's state at the moment of its intensest experience—and more, far more beside ; not merely the realisation of its most sacred personal aspirations, but the fulfilment of dearest joys and purest loves in which others are involved, nay, the fulfilment of the supreme intimacy, the white stone whereon the new name is written that no man knoweth saving Him that gives and him that doth receive. Compared with that great ultimate Reality of Life, made sure to Christian faith, it is this present life of ours that is the dream. Earth is but the lowly nursery, the dim sleeping-chamber in God's great house of many mansions. And Death but the last of earth's veiled servants of the Realm of God—

> No spectre grim,
> But just a dim
> Sweet face.

Death is but the disannulling of some of the barriers which separate us from the fuller enjoyment of the life in God.

> Death with the might of his sunbeam
> Touches the flesh and the soul *awakes*.

"As for me, I will behold Thy face in righteousness; I shall be satisfied when I awake with Thy likeness."

v

We have been trying to apprehend, in broken and half-guessed lineaments, the great religious argument for immortality as it was envisaged in the mind of Jesus. Put briefly it amounts to this. It is by the human soul's experience of fellowship with God here on earth that we lay claim to life unending. Come back now to the Temple Courts where Jesus stands confronting the Sadducees. Is it not precisely this argument with which He answered them, and sent them silent away? "Is not this where you go wrong?" He said. "You have completely mis-read, misunderstood your own Scriptures. You have heard God saying to Moses at the bush, I AM THE GOD OF ABRAHAM, AND THE GOD OF ISAAC, AND THE GOD OF JACOB, and you have failed to realise that He who was solitary Abraham's friend, and Isaac's piteous helper, and Jacob's patient guide—the God of Bethel's lonely hillside—can never cease to be their friend. That would amount to an abrogation of all the bliss which constitutes the very life of God. God is not the God of dead people, but of living men! Yea, of all sorts of men : the God of all the Abrams—the pilgrim adventurers who dream of a city that hath sure foundations, and set out into the unknown on their quest, to find their dream fulfilled at last—in God ; God of the Isaacs—the unassertive, sickly, and retiring souls, who yearn for healing from their ineffectiveness and brokenness, and find it— when they find at last their nook, in God ; God of the Jacobs, the truant, crooked souls who wander till the darkness sends them Home. They are not dead —they still live—in HIM !

"You do not understand the Scriptures," Jesus said, " do not understand what the long story of your race's intercourse with God, what the deepest experience of the great saints of your Faith—really implies. How can you be so blind to what it means that " with God "—with such a God—" is the fountain of life " ? Why is it that " in His light " you have failed to " see light " ? Nay, you do not understand the Scriptures ! And we may be sure that Jesus, who was brought up as a youth in the circle of the Hasidim, was thinking of the passages which were the special delight of those quiet, reverent homes where the flame of vital religion was kept alight, thinking of the sacred songs which the Hasidim loved to sing, yea, and perhaps quoting to those confortable, well-fed materialists who by a strange irony had become the stewards of the people's faith, this great and thrilling record of a pious soul's experience : " I have set the Lord always before me ; because He is at my right hand I shall not be moved. Therefore my heart is glad and my glory rejoiceth ; my flesh also shall rest in hope. For Thou wilt not leave my soul in the Death-regions ; neither wilt Thou suffer Thy holy one (thy ' Hasid '—me with whom Thou hast had such *hesed*, so sure a bond of mutual love) to see corruption ; Thou wilt show me the path that leads to Life. In Thy presence is fullness of joy ; at Thy right hand there are pleasures for evermore."

But side by side with that argument from experience of present fellowship to future blessedness—a present experience to which the Jewish Scriptures bore so ample testimony—Jesus set another word : " No more do you understand the power of God." And it is pertinent for our day, which has been tempted by the conception of a struggling God, to remember that Jesus never had any misgivings about God's Omnipotence. " With Him all things are possible." He it is whose Will is done in all the Realm of heaven, the Will which suns and seasons, stars and holy angels obey, and which is going to be accomplished among men on earth some day. Under no delusions as to what it cost God to accomplish His will, He nevertheless was certain of its victory. And in expanding the Saviour's thought for our present purpose, we cannot do better than quote the eloquent words of a modern teacher : "Can we conceive of God as contemplating with indifference the departure of His beloved (into nothingness at death) ? If those who have served Him most faithfully, known Him most truly, and realised the fellowship of His spirit most closely, pass away, might we not say, after the logic of our affections, that God—even God—must suffer perpetual bereavement and bury the unfulfilled promise of His creation in our graves ? And so the long procession of humanity would seem no better than a funeral train where the love of the Eternal is forever cut short by our mortal years, and the response for which He was preparing us is silent and still." It is idle to say that the mere memory of us will satisfy His heart, or that the unfulfilled ideal which He foresaw in us will console Him. "It is neither His own memory nor foresight that He loves, but the separate offspring of His might," the centres of personal life which constitute our being. "Does God call man into existence, train, discipline, judge, support, guide and inspire, and form him for communion with Himself ; and then—sever the ties He has Himself established, forgo His own work, and continually begin again the process which a cooling earth will end ? "[1] . . . It is all summed up in the pregnant line of the old English metaphysical poet :

> If they should die, then God Himself would die.

" No, no, a thousand times no ! " cries Jesus. " You, holding up your little, sorry picture of tangled earthly relationships as the contradiction and refutation of the Life Everlasting—you are far astray."

" Fear not, little flock, it is your Father's good pleasure to give you the Kingdom." " Are not two sparrows sold for a farthing ? And one of them shall not fall on the ground without your Father ; but the very hairs of your head are all numbered. Fear ye not therefore : are ye not of far more worth than sparrows ? " " Rejoice because your names are written in heaven." " The angels of little ones do always behold the face of My Father in heaven." " Blessed are the poor in spirit ; they belong to the Kingdom." " Blessed are the pure in heart ; they shall see God." " Many that are first shall be last and the last first." " To-day shalt thou be with Me in Paradise." " Father, into Thy hands I commend My spirit."

So He too tasted death at length—the last and greatest proof that God was in His life,—He who, sharing unbroken communion with God on earth, so

---

[1] J. Estlin Carpenter : The place of Immortality in Religious Belief (See *Studies in Theology* : Carpenter and Wicksteed).

felt all the agony of God's sin-pained, breaking heart that He became on the Cross God's outstretched hand to us in reconciling Forgiveness. There is our trysting place where we most surely realise the presence of God with us. Yes, apart even from His resurrection, the Cross of Jesus is the supreme instance of God's taking to do personally and individually with us men in this life, and therefore to us the most sure and solid ground on which we can rest our hope of life to come. "Through death He destroyed . . . the power of death . . . and delivered us who through fear of death were all our lifetime subject to bondage."

VI

We find ourselves standing as yet only on the threshold of this vast subject. We have merely re-stated the Christian basis of belief in immortality, glimpsed through the mind of Jesus. It would have required much more space and time to consult the mind of the Master on the moral conditions and implications of the fact of immortality. In such a further study we would have recalled how He never argued for the essential indestructibility of the soul in its own nature ; for to Him the worth and dignity of the soul—and who among the sons of men has affirmed the supreme value of human individuality as Jesus has ?—was always and solely in its relations with God the Creator.

The Mind of the Master on Immortality

We would have shown from His sayings also that, while there is a real sense in which the after-life makes compensation for the injustices and disabilities of this, the only doctrine of heavenly reward which Jesus taught was no selfish doctrine, as so many modern deniers of immortality aver, but only the more perfect opportunity for love to serve, to lose itself in sacrifice for loved ones. The Christian hope of immortality is no selfish fear of personal extinction; it is rather the

> Old belief
> That on some further shore
> Beyond earth's pain and grief,
> Dear friends will meet once more.

Heaven, in one sense, is but the Divine response to the longing of love to find ourselves eternally in the hearts of our friends.

> Eternal be the sleep
> Unless to waken so.

We think it might be argued too, that the only present communion Jesus encouraged between the dear and holy dead and us who remain behind, is not through wizards that peep and mutter, but through His own living, ever-present Spirit.

A further aspect of this subject would have to be dealt with. Jesus held the view that this earth was, indeed, as the poet Keats said, but the " vale of soul-making," the probation-span, where men by persevering faith enter at last into final and complete possession of personality.

129

Who was Jesus of Nazareth ?

And he who flagged not in the earthly strife,
  From strength to strength advancing—only he,
His soul well-knit, and all his battles won,
  Mounts, and that hardly, to eternal life.

Jesus' immediate assurance changed with the changing years. Added to the experience of immediate fellowship with God came a growing consciousness of the gulf between men and the God in Him; and a consequent sorrow and anguish, a deepening gloom of misunderstanding crept over the way, the black darkness of forsaking and Golgotha. And He began to see that this life was not merely the place where eternal life was won by communion with God, it was the place where a battle for faith was fought, where, by probation, we achieve indestructible personality. "In your patient endurance you shall win possession of your souls." It was His own experience, in the first place, His assurance of victory. His own passionate conviction that He should not remain in the realms of death, but must appear on the Day of Judgment as Lord of the future Kingdom, shows this. Out of the sense that life's vocation must be completed somewhere, sometime, comes the conviction of immortality.

And this same truth has its gloomy, reverse side. Souls can unmake themselves, straying out with careless feet to some cosmic desert of dreary exile, where their bitter weird is dreed. Yet in Jesus' view, there are provided, in the tender hospitalities of Eternity, some lowly chambers of the Father's house of many mansions, for souls whose careers were tragically thwarted and prematurely cut short on earth, souls to whom little was given and from whom little will be required. These chambers may be schoolrooms for the further education and discipline of uncompleted souls, where, gently beaten with fewer stripes, they pass from change to change, because unknowing, with dim light and blinded eyes, they wandered from the path on earth.

But, further, closely linked with this doctrine of probation, is Jesus' view that the uniqueness of each individual lies wrapped up in his purpose in life, the lot and vocation to which God has called him here ; and that his eternal place in God's great scheme is determined not by his brilliance but by his faithfulness in this earthly vocation ; that he who believes in his vocation as Antonio Stradivarius the violin maker did in his (" God could not make another of these violins without Antonio "), he who is faithful in a few things, yea, even in the least, is made ruler over many things hereafter, continues his earthly service with enlarged scope of usefulness and influence.

VII

Contenting ourselves perforce with this far-off, longing glance at these sacred regions of the wide-flung landscape of Eternity, let us end with just one hint, one symbolic picture of this Eternal life which interpenetrates and is continuous with our sojourning in this outer court of the Father's house of many mansions. For it is a picture which comes, we are fain to believe, in the last resort from the Master Himself, when He spoke His assured conviction that His own earthly vocation must be completed somewhere, sometime, in the company of all His faithful ones.

In the great New Testament documents of Christian experience, the writings of Paul and the Apostles, there are two striking symbols of the communion of saints in the life everlasting, bequeathed to us. One is the picture of the company of believers alive upon the earth or already passed into the Nearer Presence, as together forming the "Mystical Body" of our Redeemer, in which His glorified soul now dwells. And the other is that of the great Temple, "the Building of God not made with hands," whose stones are the lives of believers, and whose building is to go on and on till God has made the pile complete. Both come ultimately, we feel sure, from the thoughts of our Lord. And both depict this blessed communion of saints as an organic whole, a single indivisible society in which we can say of those who have crossed over, that "they without us should not be made perfect." It is with the second we are presently concerned.

Of this mighty temple of life the Builder under God is the living and exalted Lord. He who lived the life of a builder ($\dot{o}$ $\tau\acute{\epsilon}\kappa\tau\omega\nu$) in Nazareth still lives the life of a Builder in heaven. As on earth in the hidden years, so in the Unseen, that is still His vocation, only immeasurably enhanced and glorified —a Builder.

Do you hesitate over the suggestion that Peter and Paul may have had in mind the earthly calling of the Lord? Have we nothing more to go upon than this highly problematic association of ideas? Listen then to our Lord Himself. Standing in those same Temple Courts where He met and confuted the Sadducees in the closing days of the Passion Week, did He not predict victory over death in one sentence so arresting that His enemies trumped it up against Him when He stood in bonds before the High Priest's Chair? The exact form is uncertain : John says it was : " Destroy this Temple and in three days I will build it up again." From Mark we would gather that it was the building of another " Temple, made without hands," He predicted. " He spake of the Temple of His body," says John ; yes, but we may take Mark's word for it that it was not the body of His flesh. It was the Mystical Body in which the lives of all the faithful are to find their place. This surely was the enduring Temple He was to rear when the ancient shrine of Jewry was levelled to the ground, and all its sacrifices of slain beasts had passed away. It is built upon the foundation of the Apostles and Prophets, the Builder Himself being the chief Corner stone, which other builders vainly building had despised. Thus speaks Paul. And Peter, writing to his followers, says,

Who was Jesus of Nazareth?

"When ye come to Him, ye also, as lively stones, are built up, a spiritual house. . . by Jesus Christ." And when it is remembered that both of them refer to the stone which the builders rejected, a word which the Builder of Nazareth had also recalled in the Temple Courts, that fateful week, we seem to be carried irresistibly back to Jesus as the source of the conception.

Do we still doubt and hesitate? Listen once again to the Builder speaking His soaring word to this very Peter who had just confessed His name at Caesarea Philippi: "Thou art Peter, and on this rock will I build my Church, and the gates of Death shall not prevail against it." Yes, still to-day—we have His own word for it—He is Eternity's great Builder, "in whom all the building fitly framed together groweth unto an holy temple in the Lord: in whom ye also are builded together for an habitation of God through the Spirit."

VII.

What is now meant by the Authority of Scripture

ONE outstanding feature of life to-day is its masterlessness. And this is true of practically every phase of it,—commerce, industry, politics, art, science, philosophy, morals, religion. We have loosed from the old moorings, but, for the ordinary mariner, the charts of the great sea have been lost or destroyed. We are bewildered and can take no bearings. We are suffering from loss of authority.

The anarchy, the revolutionary spirit which is abroad, has a praiseworthy element at the root of it. It is a passion for life, and the freedom which is life's crown and joy. But freedom is not the end of life. The end of life lies in the Purpose and Will of God. There only is true freedom found. The passion for life can only be satisfied in the Lord and Giver of life. This is Life's supreme Authority by which all other authorities are finally determined.

The question of the supreme religious authority is, of course, a wider one than that of the authority of Scripture. But the two are intimately bound up with each other. For the main problem about the abiding authority in religion to-day is precisely as to its point of impact upon human life. And the question of Scriptural authority is an integral part of that problem. How may the voice of God reach again the heart and conscience of mankind ? In face of the undermining of all other forms of authority, must we be content with affirming the autonomy of the conscience ? " Stern daughter of the voice of God," sang Wordsworth of Duty :

Thou dost preserve the stars from wrong,
And the most ancient heavens, through thee, are fresh and strong.

But the trouble is that we cannot say "the Kingdom of Humanity, through Thee, is fresh and strong." Bishop Butler said of the conscience : " Had it might as it has right it would absolutely govern the world." But civilisation is broken ; human society is bankrupt. We are more conscious than ever to-day of lack of purity and lack of power. If God had left conscience to fight its battle alone, this would be of all worlds the most miserable. But the Scripture records declare that the Divine voice *has* uttered itself in human history. The authority of these records is therefore a question of fundamental importance in determining the nature of the Divine impact upon the soul of man.

I

A few historical notes may help to remind us of the nature and ramifications of the question at issue.

In nearly every period of the Church's history it has been maintained with more or less persistency

The Authority of Scripture

that Christianity is a religion of the Spirit, not a book religion. Christianity lived, and the fellowship of the faith expanded rapidly, for almost a generation, without the aid of any specifically Christian document; and for three centuries, more or less, without a universally recognised canon of Christian Scripture. Nevertheless, owing to the frailty of human nature, the attempt of the fellowship to live the life of the Spirit without leaning on extraneous authority has always been found as difficult as trying to maintain an unstable equilibrium. And the tendency to repose in external authority has oscillated between Apostolic tradition as embodied in ecclesiastical organisation on the one hand, and Apostolic authority as embodied in documents on the other. The passing of the first generation of Christ's followers and the growth of heresy led to the recognition of both these organs of authority. Indeed the ability of the heretics to quote or invent Apostolic documents in their own support led men like Papias to go behind the documents to Apostolic tradition as the prior authority. And by and by the Church, as the heir of Apostolic tradition, constituted herself as the final arbiter not only of the limits of the Canonical writings, but of their interpretation. Mediævalism crystallised this into a dogma. "*Ego uero euangelio non crederem,*" said St. Augustine, "*nisi me Catholicae ecclesiae commoueret auctoritas.*" (I indeed would not believe the Gospel, unless the authority of the Catholic Church moved me along with it.)

One of the main results of the Reformation was to shift the weight of authority, for Prostestant Christianity, from the Church to the Bible, from an infallible Pope to an infallible Book, which a Roman critic of the Reformation called 'the paper Pope of the Protestants.' Such a summing up of Church History is, however, only a cursory and superficial view of the situation. Far behind the Reformation lies another decisive moment in the history of this question. Recently Harnack, with a wealth of erudition, has gone far to establish the thesis that the most important figure between St. Paul and St. Augustine is Marcion. Before Marcion, there were Churches but no Church Catholic, documents but no New Testament. We owe both of these facts, not to Marcion indeed, but to the reaction against Marcion. Yet the appearance of Marcion forms an epoch in the life of Christianity.

Now it is not exactly true to say that before Marcion Christianity was a bookless religion. From the beginning, as the New Testament writings themselves witness, the Jewish Christian fellowship regarded the Old Testament as a book of Divine authority. According to Dr. Rendell Harris's recent investigations, the earliest writings engaged in by Christians were compilations of Messianic Oracles from the Old Testament. And the impulse of the early Church was right, if the method was faulty.

The Authority of Scripture

It is partly in tracing the growth of the Messianic idea that the Old Testament is still valuable to us to-day. It was, however, concerning the Old Testament that the first serious assault was made on the authority of Scripture—and by Marcion. And it is noteworthy that it came, not along the line of textual but of ethical criticism. That the God of the Old Testament was not the God of the New, sounds a fantastic speculation to us to-day. The Faith, whose creed was, " Hear, O Israel, the Lord our God, the Lord is one," had already in principle transcended that view. The monotheism of the prophets forms the starting-point for the New Testament revelation. But it is the failure of the Church to adjust its views against the strength of Marcion's attack that has made the ethical assault on the Old Testament assume such grave dimensions to-day.

The failure of the Church took, first, the direction of a hardening of the dogma of plenary inspiration. The Jewish Christian Church not only adopted the Old Testament as Scripture, but adopted the attitude which the Jewish hierarchy maintained to their Scriptures as well. It cannot be too strongly asserted that the doctrine of plenary inspiration is a Jewish, not an intrinsically Christian doctrine. It was fashioned in the inter-Testamental period, and was taken over by the Church from the Synagogue. When the Massorete wiped his pen and took a fresh dip of ink every time he copied the sacred Name, it is a witness to the superstition of the Jew concerning the explosive force for good or evil stored up in words. The very errors of earlier copyists were sacred to the Massoretes. Inspiration was regarded as uniform, mechanical and equal in every part. Every word and every letter had an absolutely binding force. And it was a deepening of disaster when the same doctrine came to be held concerning the New Testament writings.

Again, the determining of the limits of the Canon became a pressing problem after Marcion. The authority of the Canon is a somewhat different question from the authority of Scripture. It would not be quite fair to say the authority of Scripture is from God, the authority of the Canon, from the Church. But the authority of Scripture speaks from within Scripture, direct to heart and conscience. The authority of the Canon is an ecclesiastical rule imposed more or less from without. Yet the two things have this connection : the latter is an attempt to decree by ecclesiastical fiat which writings do speak to us with the authentic voice of God. The challenge has often been made, whether any sort of spiritual authority can be acknowledged in a decison of Council in which logic was helped out by clamour and even by fists, and a result reached by vote of the majority. Is this the way in which the guidance of the Holy Spirit operates ? In fairness, three things must be set down by way of rejoinder. When one compares the documents of the New Testament with the patristic writings, and recognises the astonishing difference in the level of spiritual illumination ; when one remembers also that in the nineteen centuries which have elapsed, no great Christian writing has appeared which does not owe all its greatness to the New Testament, one is compelled to admit that the verdict of the Church was substantially right. Secondly, we have to remember that the limits of the Canon were virtually determined long before any decree of Council, by the growing consensus of the Christian community. Thirdly, it will be freely acknowledged that no decree of Council could have voted a secular book, or even a religious book of indifferent value, that had not the Apostolic imprimatur, to a place within the canon. It must first authenticate itself as speaking from God to the heart and conscience of the Christian community. Even the Roman communion admits that the soul with its inner testimony of the Spirit is the ultimate seat of authority. In the light of these considerations we do right to acknowledge the Church's guidance by the Holy Spirit in fixing the Canon of Scripture. The Church's failure here lay in not adding the necessary proviso. It is the Church of the saints, not the Church of the hierarchy, that has spiritual authority. The true Apostolic succession is the succession of the faithful. And the heart and conscience of the living Church of believers must still hold themselves free to make their own Spirit-guided judgments as to the nature and degree of the authority of Scripture within the Canon.

But the Church of the hierarchy took a further false step in the centuries succeeding the age of Marcion. It arrogated to itself the function of arbiter of dogma. It was soon found that it was not sufficient to define the Canon as the sole source for Christian truth. The heterodox became just as nimble at discovering his own doctrine in Scripture as the orthodox. There was a deal of bandying of texts at Nicea. But the determining of dogma by the Church became a tyranny. Every great renewal of the Church's life was partly of the nature of a revolt against this tyranny. The Reformation was such. And it was not, in the first instance, the exchange of one set of dogmata for another. It was a rediscovery of the fontal religious experience which lies behind all dogma. Yet when the first wave of spiritual quickening passed, the old struggle over dogma began again ; until the squib of Werenfels of Basel became true :

> Hic liber est in quo quærit sua dogmata quisque,
> Inuenit et pariter dogmata quisque sua.

(This is the book in which everyone tries to find his own dogmas. And what are the doctrines each finds ? Just precisely his own.)

The attempt to buttress the authority of Scripture by the authority of the Church led to a displacing of the one by the other to the detriment of both. And long before the Reformation the first whispers of a new assault on the infallibility of Scripture were beginning to be audible. The discovery of endless variants gradually undermined the theory of plenary textual inspiration. From the days of Pope Damasus and St. Jerome, the Church has felt the need of meeting that difficulty. An attempt was made to establish the true text, or a text which should be universally received as such, an attempt not merely by the Roman Church but by the Reformed Church as well. A note in the Preface of one of the Elzevir editions of the New Testament— " *Textum nunc habes ab omnibus receptum* "—had almost more influence in determining the text for the Church of the Reformation than the decree of the Council of Trent had in establishing a corrupt version of the Vulgate for Rome. It was said of the Council of Trent that the Spirit came from Rome in fetters. But a boastful note in an editor's preface can scarcely be said to have a better claim to be the voice of the Spirit. And neither decree nor preface stayed the researches of scholars. Which among the 150,000 variant readings were the true ones of this infallible book ? Such was the next big assault upon the authority of Scripture, or at least upon the theory of plenary textual inspiration.

A few sentences will suffice to describe the present-day, many-sided assault upon the authority of Scripture—the result of scientific research both in things secular and in things sacred. Copernicus, Galileo, Newton, Kelper removed—for human thought—the earth from the centre of the universe; Darwin turned the creation story into myth and poetry; the literary and historical critics have called in question the authenticity, accuracy and integrity of the Scripture documents. The results of their labours have broken out like a flood from the narrow cloisters of scholarship and poured along the ordinary ways of human intercourse. And the fetish of an infallible book, inspired in every word, lies in hopeless ruins.

The old symbols of the hand beckoning out of heaven, the heavenly book that is eaten and then retold by the recorder's pen, the dove whispering in the ear, the Divine ray shining on the head of the evangelist whose hand extends in benediction over his amanuensis (as in the quaint old etching of St. John and Prochorus)—these have to be set aside. Even the figures of the human lyre played upon by the fingers of God, of the flute breathed through by the Holy Spirit, of men as the hands and pens of the Holy Ghost, who is sole author—these too have to be abandoned. The idea of Divine Guidance, *in actu scribendi*, of a mere passive, Divinely hypnotised medium, is untenable. It is men with all their human faculties active, all their idiosyncrasies in full play, men beset by all their earthly frailties and limitations, that are inspired—not written words. " God," says C. H. Dodd in his recent book on the Authority of the Bible, " is the author not of the Bible but of the life in which the authors of the Bible partake, and of which they tell in such imperfect human words as they could command."

"Inspiration," he says again, "does not carry inerrancy, nor is it inerrancy that gives authority." These men are inspired to teach neither science, philosophy, nor history, but to record the authentic drawing near of God to men in history. And it is as such the writings still make their appeal to us. The writers are men lifted up to share in a great religious experience as they react to the intervention of God in human history. And it is to *our* spiritual faculties, our religious instinct, our faith, our religious experience they make their appeal. "Nothing is ours, however it be presented to us," says Principal Oman, "except we discover its truth, and except it prove itself again in our experience."

II

How then shall we begin again to reconstruct our view of the authority of Scripture ? And what should the nature of that authority be ?

Two principles—sanctioned in Reformation theology—form our starting-point : the principle that the Word of God is not the letter of Scripture, but is contained in Scripture ; and the correlated principle, that the judge of what constitutes the Word of God in Scripuure is the *Testimonium internum Spiritus sancti.* But the Word of God and the inner testimony of the spirit are in themselves almost abstractions. We must find some concrete,

145

unifying point of view from which we may formulate a doctrine of the authority of Scripture. Otherwise the inward witness of the Spirit may easily become for us the soul's natural light that lighteth every man coming into the world, which may be anything from the Socratic *daimonion*, or the Inner Light of Quakerism, to the conscience. And the Word of God may come to be sought for in dim, vague insights, not merely in the Bible but also in nature and the science of nature, in the sacred writings of other faiths, and in the classic literature of all the world. Doubtless some " word of God " is to be found there. God writes upon the veil that hides His face ; God writes His law upon the heart of pagans, " their conscience also bearing witness, and their thoughts the meanwhile accusing or else excusing one another " ; He " hath nowhere left Himself without a witness." But for Christian faith, these do not constitute *the* Word of God, nor is it *before* the Word, but *by* and *with* the Word that the Holy Spirit witnesses in our hearts.

In what way, then, may we link the Word with the inner Witness so as to avoid these errors ? To put the matter briefly, in three or four defining sentences : *Scripture*, for the Christian believer, is the record of the one central and supreme, Divine, revelatory process and its consummation in human history. And the authoritative *Word* of God in Scripture is the Gospel of the choosing, saving, and redeeming God in action which culminates in the

The Authority of Scripture

Cross of Christ. "God," says Dodd, "touches us supremely in the literature of the Bible. . . . because the experience these writings transmit is so organically related to history and to the Divine Incarnation in Christ, in which we recognise the supreme act of God in history." And the inner *Witness* of the Spirit is simply the believer's experience of the impact of this Gospel on his soul. It is there, in "the word of the Cross," as it meets with, and apprehends, our spirits that the authority of Scripture lies for us, because *there* is the Divine act that utters and reveals the supreme purpose of the Divine Will.

There is nothing prior to this experience for the Christian. For the Church is the creation of the Gospel and of the experience which flows from the Gospel; the Book is the expression of the experience. Nor is the experience merely subjective. The seat of authority is in experience : the source and the throne of it is in God. That which we call faith in us, is, in essence, the same thing in the sacred writers, only raised to the level of inspiration. What, in our case, is the being apprehended by God in the Cross of Christ is, in the case of the sacred writers, the being commissioned by God to convey the Gospel revelation. The Word and the inner witness are, we might say, the objective and the subjective aspects of the one supreme fact of Experience.

That condensed statement may be illustrated and expanded in this way. When Mr. H. G. Wells essays to fashion a new Bible for us, by constructing a thesaurion or anthology from the books of the greater religions and the world's classics, he has missed the essential significance of what it is that constitutes a Bible. The result of his labours might, indeed, be a record of man's spiritual development, but it would not be a record of God's taking action in history for one supreme, redemptive end. It is God active to this end in history that is the soul's only religious authority. And it is the record of this redemption activity that constitutes our sole Bible.

Nor is it any contradiction of this when we say that the one authority to which the soul can bow, uttering its consenting " Amen," is the inner testimony of the Spirit. For the Christ on His Cross is the ultimate and supreme gateway through which the Spirit now comes to man in the experience of redemption. The seat of authority, we have said, is the soul, but the source is God. And the channel from the source to this inner well which springs up into everlasting life is the Gospel. The experience is God stooping down to reach man, met by man reaching up to God, in the Gospel. "The criterion lies within ourselves, in the response of our own spirit to the Spirit that utters itself in the Scriptures." Not man in his solitude, be it said, lest we be thought to minimise the place of the Church in this experience, but the believer within the Fellowship of Faith, a member of the Mystical Body, the Church Catholic. For the witness which is valid from age to age goes back to the Person of Christ, and to Christ on His Cross, " not through the void, but through the peace and joy and holiness He has wrought in the souls of men." And the unique and fontal expression of that experience is, and must ever remain, the Scriptures. " Authority," says Principal Forsyth, " speaks in experience, especially the corporate experience of the Church, and the classic expression of that experience is in the Canonical documents of our faith."

III.

How does the view here indicated apply to the different phases of " the classic expression of that experience ? "

It is no inversion of the true order, but in the nature of things, that we begin with the New Testament, and with the Gospels in the New Testament. The Gospels are for us the records of the redeeming Passion of our Lord. They are born out of the Christian experience, which still lives in the Church, in the bosom of which we receive them. Love still finds its Galilee in the Gospels, and faith its Calvary and Olivet. When the Passion of our Lord speaks home to us in the experience of faith, we find ourselves on a rock remote from the sapping tides of critical science. For the Gospels are testimonies to Christ borne by the first believers, and only in a secondary sense histories about Christ. When Christ is thus held up to us, the voice of God becomes, not only audible, but significant and compelling in Him. And "it is by no means necessary that we should know everything that is in the Gospels to be true, or that we should be bound to the accuracy of every detail, before they begin to do for us what God designs them to do. . . . It is to Christ we give our trust, and as long as the Gospels make us sure of what He is, they serve God's purpose and our need" (Denney). Nay, if we accept the dictates of the Spirit we must be prepared to go all the length with truth. No truth can be alien to The Truth, into the freedom of which we have been promised guidance.

If the Gospels have authority as the record of the Passion of Christ, what of the Epistles? Are they not simply the expressed opinions of other believers—among the first generation, it is true, but still just believers on the same level of faith as our own? Is the important thing, as Herrmann affirms, not that we should have the thoughts of the Apostles about Christ, but that we should have our own? Surely the important thing is that we should have *God's* thoughts about Christ. And does it not stand to reason that if God's action in history consummated itself as fact and life in Jesus Christ, God must add another chapter to His book of revelation, to disclose the full meaning of that fact and that life; and that chapter must follow immediately upon the appearance of the fact, if His revelation is not to be lost to the world? Once more, God's

The Authority of Scripture

Word in the Apostolic testimony, witnessing with the inner testimony of the Spirit, convinces us that these Apostolic witnesses are the Divinely appointed human mirrors in which the great redemption fact is not only reflected, but made to yield up its inner secrets for the sake of a perishing world. The Gospels manifest God's Deed in history : the Epistles are its inspired interpretation. They are not a light shed on the fact from outside ; they are a liberating of the radiance which belongs to the fact. They are the ever-living fact, speaking in its God-appointed, final, and normative expression. Gospel and Epistles together form the record of the one supreme religious fact, which is the Lord, the Spirit. Speaking in the Apostles, the Spirit is the expositor and translator of what the Lord has done. The Apostles were uniquely and Divinely commissioned for the task ; they are the human intermediaries of God's mind expressed once in the fact, and again in the glory that breaks from the fact. The act is inseparable from its own account of itself, through men raised up for the purpose. No doubt they had to express it in the language of the thought-moulds of the age. But the Spirit speaking in the Word and in the heart of the believer is Itself Its own judge to separate form from content.[1]

What is the significance of the Old Testament in this point of view ? Suppose our Lord Jesus, and the Christian experience, and the New Testament

[1] See P. T. Forsyth : *Principle of Authority.*

had never come into existence : would the Scriptures of the Old Testament have become documents of Divine authority for so great a portion of mankind ? We venture to suggest they would have remained little more than the Scriptures of the Jews. On the other hand, suppose the Old Testament, and the history, the experience behind the Old Testament, had never been : would the New Testament revelation have made anything like its full and far-flung impact upon the world ? Would it, indeed, have been possible for the New Testament revelation to begin just where it did ? Without the mountain-mass of Old Testament monotheism, could the stainless peak of New Testament revelation have risen up into the full blaze of God's sunlight ? Only by a violation of the law of progressive revelation. And because of the limitations of human nature it would have failed. We would have been unprepared for it. The inspiration of the New Testament forms an organic unity with the Old. The authority of the Old Testament for the Christian is dependent on the Divine authority of the Gospel. The Old Testament Scriptures are the record of an integral and preparatory part of the Divine Action in History, —the record of the gradual and progressive disclosure of the mind and will of God for man. Under the old mechanical view of verbal inspiration, the Old Testament is full of stumbling-blocks for the morally awakened and Christ-enlightened mind. It is the principle of the progressiveness of revelation that clears away the difficulty. And surely the time has come for us to teach it publicly, if not in season and out of season, at least on all timely and appropriate occasions.

In saying so we are not claiming the right of private judgment to pronounce criticism on the morals of the older dispensation. We measure the relative dimness or brightness of the Old Testament insights by the full flood of the Gospel theophany. Above all, in the handling of the Old Testament Scriptures, the example of our Lord must ever hold the place of supreme authority for the Christian. The loss of authority within the Church to-day is in part a Nemesis for our misunderstanding and misinterpretation of His reverence for the sacred books of Israel, and for our failure to follow Him in His fearless freedom. If we examine His references to the Old Testament with a view to determining His principle of selection, we find that His criticism of the details of the Mosaic Law was ever in the light of the highest that the Law itself contained. Again, about practically every one of the incidents of Old Testament history He refers to, the remarkable feature is that they represent some veritable drawing near of God to man. And His favourite Psalms, the prophetic words He chooses, are those that have this also for their burden, or those that shine with the brightest light of heaven. The heart of all the Law, for Him, is love to God and man. The heart of history is the drawing near of God to man. The heart of prophecy is the mercy of God to man, and the Divine Law of suffering service. It belongs to the uniqueness of Christ that it was He who identified the Messiah of expectation with God's suffering Servant of prophecy, and found that supreme purpose of God for man's redemption being realised in Himself. It is there, surely, there above all else, that the focal point of the authority of the Old Testament Scriptures lies for us to-day.

VIII

The Spirit of God, and the New Testament Experience

ONE thing the tragedy of the great and terrible years of the War did for us : it freed us from the thraldom of a false view of progress.   Our complacent picture of a gradual and unbroken amelioration of society is shattered.   We cannot, indeed, surrender our faith in a holy purpose working itself out through history to its predestined goal.   But it is now evident that evil and good alike move towards climaxes, and periodically crash together in vast and blinding catastrophes.   Out of these, new world-orders emerge.   In short, the march of mankind seems to proceed upward along a spiral stairway, round which we swing from light to dark, from dark to light.

There are times and seasons of moral and spiritual ebb and flow in the story of the spirit of man. Times of long slumber separate the times of awaking. There is, in history, a Divine wisdom and economy of recipient waiting.   Some ages must lie fallow that others may richly yield.   When the surface life of the soul becomes crusted over by traditionalism, false thinking, bad government, the fires of the Divine Spirit seethe underground, storing up their energies against the day of eruption.

Sometimes the advent of the liberating thought is achieved through the dim groping of the group-soul. But individuals are the true vocal concentration-points within the life of the Spirit in which we live and move and have our being ; and so it is more natural that the age or society which has grown sensitive to the deeper harmonies of Reality should express itself through individual listeners, who have in finer balance these spiritual faculties which are common to mankind. It is through these sometimes very lonely men, who feel and see the same Spirit which is stirring within their own souls, moving upon the face of the waters of the world, who keep the memory of its inarticulate cries, " half-guessed and gone again," and who ponder them in their hearts, that this Divine Life at last breaks into soaring utterance, bringing out of three sounds " not a fourth sound but a star." And these inspired voices echo and re-echo through the sensitive society wherein they arise, still further heightening and enhancing its sensitiveness, and awakening answering voices there. They are the God-sent Answerers to the questionings of the day, the Knights of the Spirit, who smite with the sword of light against the opposing darkness, and clear the path for progress.

The proof of this is apparent in history. Always

the times of national and world-upheaval have
coincided more or less with the times when the
world's heart has been stirred into noblest utterance.
" The glory that was Greece " gleams with most
radiant lustre out of one brief century—the same
century which compasses the Ionic Revolt, and the
Persian Wars, and which saw the supremacy of
Athens.   There, in the Age of Pericles, are set the
names of Aeschylus, Sophocles, Euripides, Aristo-
phanes, Herodotus and Thucydides ; Plato and
Aristotle. " The grandeur which was Rome "—the
later days of the Republic—glitter with the names
of Caesar, Sallust, Cicero, Lucretius, Virgil, Horace,
Ovid, Livy—a galaxy close-packed into forty years of
time.   Take an equally short space of time out of
the heart of the European Renaissance, and you will
find it scintillating with the names of Machiavelli,
Columbus, Paracelsus, Copernicus, Leonardo da
Vinci, Raphael, Michael Angelo, Luther, Calvin,
John Knox, Erasmus, Loyola, Francis Xavier,
Santa Teresa.   One does not need to repeat the
names of " the spacious days of great Elizabeth "
to prove that the age of mighty doings was also an
age of lofty voices. The days of mid-Europe's
Sturm und Drang were also the days significantly
known as Germany's *Blüte-zeit*, when in one single
century she gave to the world Lessing, Herder,
Goethe, Schiller, Kant, Fichte, Schelling, Hegel,
Schopenhauer, von Hartmann, Richter, the two
Schlegels, Schleiermacher, Heine.

Who was Jesus of Nazareth ?

In the history of Religion we find the same Law at work. Often, indeed, a great religious movement is part and parcel of a wider upsurging of spiritual forces. The Reformation may be said to be part of the broad stream of the Renaissance, a freshening of the current in its later decades. The nobler spirits of the great day of Greece—Plato and the tragic dramatists—were also voices of religious reform. Israel had her prophets in the days of her national exaltation ; she had her prophets who heralded, and by-and-by voiced, the sorrows and hopes of the exile ; she had her prophets of the restoration.

It was in obedience to the same divine Law of Periodicity that our Christian Faith and the literature it produced were born. It was out of a great experience in just such an " appointed time " that the New Testament sprang. And here too we remind ourselves that it was all written within about one hundred years after the beginning of that experience. The first of Paul's letters was written only twenty years after the Crucifixion ; the Fourth Gospel probably about seventy. Thus, if we do not take into the reckoning the two or three later documents—those, indeed, in which we witness the ebbing of the tide of the Spirit, the tendency to lean on earlier utterances,—*all* the great creative literature of the New Testament was written within a space of about fifty years.

The Spirit of God, and the N.T. Experience

II. THE SOURCE OF THE NEW TESTAMENT EXPERIENCE

What was this experience ?   Whence came it ?
If we were to make the four Gospels coalesce into a
single account of the story they each claim to tell,
and were then to place the Book of *Acts* as a background for most of the Epistolary part of the New
Testament, a cursory glance would reveal to us the
fact that there are two great waves of spiritual life
to be found in the experience out of which the New
Testament came—the first being the deep, soul-
moving impression which the Supreme Personality
of Jesus made on His followers in the days of His
flesh, and the second being the excitement and
zealous propagandism which followed Pentecost.
And the consistent testimony of this second phase
of the experience is, that it was due to none other than
the re-asserted personality of the Lord, in a risen,
death-conquering life beyond the Cross.   There
can be no question as to the avowed fountain-head
of the entire New Testament experience.   It was
the entrance into human history of Jesus Christ
our Lord.

He came at the end of a dreary stretch of fallow
ground in the pilgrimage of Israel.   He was born
into a race which had a unique religious history.
The great inheritance of monotheism was the
mountain, climbing which, He reached His unparalleled vision.   And He came to be God's Answer
to a world-wide awakening and yearning after
redemption, visible in all the cults and mystery-

faiths which were vainly trying to supply man's need. He was not isolated from His environment. For all this preparation, this waiting with growing expectancy, this stirring of the dormant spirit of man, this awaking and yearning, was nothing less than the Spirit of the Most High overshadowing the age to bring to the birth what He had desired, and planned, and toiled for, in mankind. Nevertheless, Christ stands alone in history. He is absolutely without compeer or coadjutor in the creation of the New Testament experience.

St. Paul and St. John have sometimes been set alongside of Him, if not even above Him, as co-founders of the Christian religion. That is to violate the inmost sanctities of these great souls. St. Paul carried abroad the torch of his faith, " determined to know nothing among " those to whom he spoke " but Jesus Christ and Him Crucified." " For him to live was Christ." And the Christ St. John proclaims in his Gospel is the Christ who says, " Abide in me. . . . Without Me ye can do nothing." As the source of the entire New Testament experience Jesus stands alone.

III. CHRISTIANITY VIEWED AS AN AMALGAM

Yet another view has sometimes been taken of the source of the New Testament experience, which would reduce the influence of personality to a minimum. In a book entitled *The Beginnings of Christianity*, published a few years ago by well-known scholars, it is asserted that " like all religions . . . Christianity is a process, not a result." This, they say, is the view of critical study. It is a curiously uncritical and unguarded statement. Our Christian Faith should, indeed, be likened to a stream, rather than to a lake born of deep springs. Nor will anyone deny that it has gathered much that is good, and not a little that is bad, in its course through the centuries. But the fact that the stream had a fountain-head is belittled in the volume we have quoted. Surely it is just as true of historical as of geographical watersheds, that the main direction of the stream is determined by the initial outflow from the springs. But, further, Christianity is a force, rather than a " process." It determines and regulates the process. It has the power, not only to attract what is true, (for no truth is alien to " The Truth "), but ultimately to repel what has no vital affinity with it. Like the waters of the stream, Christianity is a purifying force. In the Councils of Nicea and Chalcedon we see that force—however imperfectly —at work. And when we come to the Reformation, our eyes are opened to the *method* by which the cleansing and renewing of the Faith took place. It was by a turning back to the source. It was by an unparalleled inflow from the waters of the fountain-head in the New Testament. For, undoubtedly, the life-giving waters are those which gathered and flowed in the first fifty or sixty years after Calvary. It is, therefore, New Testament

Who was Jesus of Nazareth?

Christianity which is our primary concern, not the Christianity of later accretions. The theology of the New Testament is quite different from the theology of later reflection. It is experimental from first to last—the expression and interpretation of a great experience. In so far as there is syncretism in the New Testament, it is a syncretism in which the fundamental and determining factor was the new, Divine energy which had broken into the world. Granted that it flowed into alien moulds of thought, it was not they which altered it but it which altered them, and gave them a new dimension. Where it could not do so, it speedily shattered them, burst the ancient and inadequate wine-skins, and over-flowed all their bounds. To use the other metaphor which Jesus has given us, Christianity is a self-renewing robe, not a patched garment. When these writers tell us that " the people of the Levant . . . interpreted " the new Faith "in accordance with their own thoughts rather than with its origin, thus starting a new synthesis between Judaism and the Græco-Oriental thought of the Empire," we are offered a false and foolish contrast. They interpreted the original spiritual impulse in terms of their own thought, no doubt. They could do no other. But they were not faced with a choice between their own thoughts and the Faith's origin. It was precisely the origin they interpreted in accordance with their own thoughts. They had nothing else to interpret. Rather, we should say, the new fontal experience remoulded and enlarged their own plastic moulds of thought, in its effort to find expression for itself adequate to its Divine dimensions.

IV. " BACK TO THE NEW TESTAMENT EXPERIENCE"

There has arisen to-day an urgent demand to reinterpret our faith in terms which are intelligible to our world of thought, lighted as it is with the light of far-reaching scientific discovery. Only at our peril may we ignore the lesson of history. The Faith has uttered itself in many forms. It is the very life of Faith to do so. But the experience behind them is one and constant. And we must return to its source in the New Testament, and endeavour to grasp anew the nature of that experience, if ever it is to become living and life-giving for us again. " Back to Christ " was the watchword of a generation ago ; it is sometimes said that the watchword of the present hour in religion is " Back to the Jesus of History." Surely another summons must claim priority. The only records we possess of the career of Jesus are themselves written out of the heart of the New Testament experience. It was only after the first introspective outburst of the great experience—represented by the letters of Paul—that there came the period of retrospection, the writing of the memorabilia. Doubtless in the last of them we see the experience rising to clarified and full-orbed vision of God, the world, and history in Christ. But when it opens :

Who was Jesus of Nazareth?

" In the beginning was the Word, and the Word was with God, and the Word was God. . . . And the Word was made flesh and dwelt among us," the spirit and attitude is not essentially different from that of the earliest Gospel which designates itself "The beginning of the Gospel of Jesus *Christ, the Son of God.*" "Back to the New Testament Experience " should, therefore, be our watchword to-day. Only when the fire of the New Testament Life begins to glow again for us with its full significance, shall we be able to give the right name to the flame in the heart of Christ at which the fire was kindled.

But an interpretation of the New Testament experience ?—is that anything other than a construction of New Testament Theology ? The question may be asked with a sarcastic emphasis on the word " theology." For it is fashionable to-day to disparage theology, in the interest of what is sometimes called reality—the direct contact with fact which the feelings are supposed to give. We answer that it is a bare and empty contact with reality which is won through feelings, sensations, thrills, emotions. If anything is characteristic of Reality, it is the presence of Reason and Purpose there. And until our feelings are filled with rational content and meaning, we have no contact with reality worthy of the name. After all, as has been well said, " theology is only thought applied to religion, and those who prefer a thoughtless religion

need not be so disdainful of others with a more
rationalistic taste."

Nevertheless the present-day disparagement of
theology is not without a certain justification. The
New Testament has, in the past, been too frequently
regarded as the complete, Divine revelation of
infallible and final truth given in the only perfect
form. It has been studied *in vacuo*, isolated from
history, from its social and intellectual environment,
from the temperaments of the writers. It has been
laid on the dissecting table ; its ideas sorted out and
labelled like the bones of a skeleton, the scalpels and
dissecting needles being the categories of an abstract
and alien logic. Its sentences, words, and phrases
have been manipulated into a mosaic of intellectual
dogmata. With the lapse of centuries, tradition
came to add its quota to the evil process. Thought
which is merely inherited—which is no longer the
expression of a living faith—inevitably degenerates :
the desiccated limbs of this dead body became
fossilised and crusted over with a hoary fungus,
making it hard to believe it ever was a living thing
at all.

The only way out from such a tangle is to go back
to the New Testament experience. It is of vital
moment for our human life to-day that we should
seek to do so. For the New Testament experience
was not the creation of an enchanted world, apart
from the world in which it lived. It was the
most vitalising moment of history, the loftiest

mountain-region in the whole landscape of human experience. And we have got to cut our own path up the face of the mountain, if we would renew the exhilarating contact with the life-giving, heavenly air.

V. THE NEW TESTAMENT EXPERIENCE AND ITS MODES OF EXPRESSION

One obvious way of beginning this task is by distinguishing carefully between the New Testament experience and the modes in which it expresses itself in the New Testament. And our first duty is to acknowledge that our Faith is but the consummation of God's dealings with the ancient people, who gave to the world the knowledge of the One True God. It sprang from the giant tree of this noble monotheism ; a branch or shoot springing from the buried roots of this old tree in a dry ground. Yet it is not wholly true to say that it came at a time when the old faith was almost quenched. If Christianity had sprung to life in a merely desert time of human thought, the flower of the desert would, like Mohammedanism, have borne the character of the desert. But Judaism had manifested two main lines of development—the prophetic and the legalistic. And Christianity was the consummation of the prophetic movement, the warm life of which had been kept alive by the Hasidim, " die Stillen im Lande." Christianity was a new reaction against the trammels of legalism. And it was inevitable that the form of its expression should be determined largely by that fact. St. Paul has often been accused of clothing his experience in the garments of a worn out Pharisaism. His weapons were the weapons with which the ancient faith provided him. But the battle which he fought under the banner of Christ is a battle which will always go on, so long as there is religion in the world. It is the battle between the religion of adventure and the free spirit, and the religion of externally imposed precept and ritual. In spite of its Jewish dress, the Epistle to the Galatians will ever be one of the great charters of spiritual freedom. " It marks an epoch in the history of man : it is the ever-precious document of his spiritual emancipation " (Godet). The experiences of the human soul which underlie the Epistle to the Romans are fundamental and universal experiences of human life. It is to these that the Church has ever turned in the hours of the great revivals, the renewals and refreshments of the Faith. And it is by the opening of fresh flood-gates into that fontal experience that the desert of our present life will be made to rejoice again and blossom as the rose.

It is true, also, that when Christianity began to spread in the Graeco-Roman world, it found the soul of man yearning for redemption from the futility of life, groping after contact with the Life that is eternal, unseen, Divine. It was inevitable that it should describe itself as a new mystery among *the mystery-cults* of the day, and fashion forms of expression for itself in relation to these. But it was not thereby losing contact with reality. This redemption-yearning is a fact indigenous to the human soul. Christianity did not import into itself the myth of the dying and rising god. It came as the response from the side of God, proclaiming the truth for which these dreams were fumbling and groping. " If," says the wittiest of our modern men of letters, " the Christian God really made the human race, would not the human race tend to rumours and perversions of the Christian God ? If the centre of our life is a certain fact, would not people far from the centre have a muddled version of that fact ? If we were so made that a Son of God must deliver us, is it odd that (pagans) should dream of a Son of God ? " And surely the difference is heaven-high between the religion which centres round a supreme, historic Personality as the God-given Answer to the yearnings of man, and the dreams, the myths which were the human off-spring of that yearning. Christianity did not falsify itself by proclaiming itself as the truth after which the universal soul of man was blindly groping.

Again the *Gnosticism* with which the Christian experience had to do battle at the outset, is no accidental or forgotten tendency of the human mind. It is as rife to-day as ever it was—the tendency to leave the bed-rock of history, to volatilise the facts of the faith into mere airy speculations and imaginings. Of course you will find certain traces of these speculations in the New Testament. St. Paul and the others were born into a thought-world of which these ideas were part of the *impedimenta*. But if St. Paul accepts that picture of the Unseen—the Divine Pleroma, peopled with aeons, messengers, thrones, archai, dynameis, he uses it only to assert that the Spirit of Christ was no mere ghostly aeon among the many floating in this Spirit-World, but that His Spirit fills the whole Pleroma, the Fullness of God, subjecting, dominating, disannulling all others ; and further—and this is the main point— that this exalted Being who thus fills the whole sphere of God, was no mere abstraction, no mere " Christ-spirit," but none other than the historical Jesus of Nazareth, who on earth was the express image of God, because In Him dwelt all the Fullness of the Godhead bodily. In view of all the theosophies and dilettante faiths of the day, the Christian experience can never exonerate itself from the task of proclaiming the same spiritual supremacy of Jesus.

The New Testament experience came into contact also with the spiritual *philosophy of Greece* in some of its Post-Platonic developments. The great thought-solvent of the time was the conception of the *Logos*, the uttered Wisdom, the Word, of God. It created the world, broke into light in the soul of man, has guided history, and has revealed from time to time the Mind of God, Light answering to light. Christianity was speaking in the language of the highest thought of the day when it said that the

Logos had made its supreme response to those up-flung search-lights of the human mind, in Jesus, the Light of the world, the Word made flesh. Anything less than the loftiest human thought was found by the Christian experience to be inadequate to that which it was ever striving to express. Just so, we to-day proclaim that Jesus is the roof and crown of Evolution, that which the Divine, indwelling Spirit of God in creation has been striving to achieve through the unfolding ages, God completing at last the circle of His Plan in Christ, the Way whereby men return to perfect communion with Him.

These are all phases of the effort of the New Testament experience to find articulate utterance for itself. The one historic experience abides behind them all. To the question of its origin and nature we now return.

VI. FAITH AND FELLOWSHIP—THE KEYS TO THE NEW TESTAMENT EXPERIENCE

Our point of departure here is clearly marked. It began in the little company of one hundred and twenty men and women, first followers of Jesus, who met day after day in the Upper Room, during the six weeks following Calvary, absorbed in the intense, eager, and expectant prayer, which found its consummation in Pentecost. This was the ecstatic experience which fairly launched the Church on its career down the tide of human history. We can only offer a meagre and rapid description of its main features. It is witnessed again in every great revival-movement in the Church's history. We do not disown its appearance in every solitary prophetic utterance of the Faith; yet it is in these group-manifestations that its essential nature is most fully, and usually most easily, seen. Clearly it was the liberating of a certain Power which lies hidden in the depths of the Spirit-life to which we belong, the opening of certain flood-gates through which this contagious, life-giving Power flowed in to the human soul, anointing and cheering the soiled face of human society, wherever it appeared. We may observe its main features in two of its latter-day manifestations: (a) When *Luther* stood in the dawn-light in his Benedictine cell at Erfurt, murmuring to himself, with his finger on an early page of " Romans ": " the just shall live by *faith*," he was opening the gate through which the Spirit surged into the long-tortured soul of this solitary monk who shook the world. He had become aware that this Spirit had poured, unchecked, unhindered, into the world, through the life and death of Jesus; that if only men would let themselves go in abandonment of *faith* to this God-sent reconciling stream of Life, it would carry them to the complete redemption of society, the establishment of God's Kingdom upon earth. And the Faith of Luther spread like lightning through the waiting spirit of the age. *Faith*—was the watchword of that movement.

(b) Again, when *Mazzini*, in a great hour of his

people's history, entered Rome, and "by a pure spiritual ascendancy, made a populace, demoralised by bad government and charity, rise to something of his own moral height, and dare to bear and die"— even if it *was* apart from the main stream of religious life, it was none the less a Pentecost. The soul of the city was laid captive by his spell, as he proclaimed the great dream of a universal brotherhood of humanity, to be achieved through the united spirit of his nation. That word of brotherhood, comradeship, fellowship, leaping from the kindled fire on the altar of his own heart, became the liberating word through which the Spirit-Power moved out, fusing a whole city into a corporate consciousness, a unique unity of spiritual life.

Faith and Fellowship—these are the two key facts that undo the inhibiting barriers for the resources of the Divine Life in God. They were both present at Pentecost. Faith, proclaiming Jesus as Lord, the open way between God and man, through whom God's purpose and God's desire find access to the human spirit. And Fellowship—that intercourse rooted in this common attitude to Jesus—in which all the dividing walls of individuality fall away, and a new and unique spiritual organism is formed, a corporate personality, an inward sense of oneness issuing in community of life. Through this group-soul, with its heightened consciousness, men realised the presence of the indwelling God moving in their hearts; all their powers became extraordinarily

enhanced; and the contagion of radiant personality
spread swiftly through the listening crowd.

Faith and Fellowship are the holiest capacities
of personality. They are really one, for faith is
fellowship with God. Personality has been sugges-
tively described as "capacity for fellowship." Sainthood, it might be said, is the apotheosis of personality,
for it is the genius for *spiritual* fellowship. Thomas
Traherne felt this passion of Fellowship and expressed it in words aglow with its fire :

O Lord, the children of my people are Thy peculiar treasures,
Make them mine, O God . . . Give me eyes
To see the beauty of that life and comfort
Wherewith those by their actions inspire the nations. . . .
When I consider, O Lord, how they come unto Thy Temples, fill
      Thy Courts, and sing Thy praises
O how wonderful they then appear !

What Stars,
Enflaming Suns,
Enlarging Seas
  Of Divine Affection,
Confirming Patterns,
Infusing Influence,
  Do I feel in these !
Who are the shining light
Of all the land (to my very soul :)
  Wings and Streams
  Carrying me unto Thee,
  The Sea of Goodness from whence they came.

Sainthood is incomplete in the anchorite ; he has
renounced human fellowship in the interests of
fellowship with God. But the unlimited thing in

the personality of Christ was His capacity for fellow-ship, not only with God but with man. The new creation of fellowship at Pentecost was the work of Christ's personality, re-asserting itself beyond the Cross, making for itself a new Body on the earth. The Holy Spirit in Christian experience was the all-inclusive, immanent Personality of God making realised contact with, and exerting His loving Will for Holiness in, the spirit of man, through Christ.

This phenomenon of Pentecost had been known to some extent before in the history of Israel. Under the inspiration of a great prophet men were some-times exalted, on wings of fire, to noble service. And they said, " If only men could always live like that, —if only this Something in the prophet could be-come the common possession of the race ! " " Would God that all the Lord's people were prophets ! " The prophet Joel voiced this yearning of democracy ; and, resting his claim on the Divine character, con-fidently affirmed that it would come true. Peter declared that it had come true—at Pentecost. " This is that which was spoken of by the prophet Joel." It was the realisation of the Spirit's presence in the corporate consciousness. All the Lord's people had become prophets. The sons and the daughters prophesied. The young men had visions and the old men dreamed dreams. It was

The vision, vision, vision of the poets—
Democratised.

The Spirit of God, and the N.T. Experience

THE SIGNIFICANCE OF THE FELLOWSHIP IN THE
NEW TESTAMENT.

It is usual to describe the new thing, created in
human society by the Holy Spirit of God, as the
Church. But it was not the external organisation
which we know in history and tradition : it was the
Communion of Saints that was the Holy Spirit's
creation. It was prior to the organised *Ecclesia*—
the Holy Catholic Church. It was "the Holy
Assembly," that invisible Spirit-organism which lies
behind all the numerous Churches, schools of tradition and doctrine, *ecclesiolae in Ecclesia*—yes, and
behind every other movement outside the Church,
whether of individuals or groups, making for the
redemption of society. When Luke first describes
it (in *Acts*), he has no other name for it but
"The Fellowship" (ἡ κοινωνία). When he tries
to describe the life of the Fellowship, the inner
impulse, the unifying motive, he can only stammer
and stumble : it was a "devoting themselves to the
Fellowship," a "continuing with one accord," a
"holding together of believers," a being "of one
heart and one mind." And—finally abandoning the
attempt at description—he says, "The Lord added
to this Something daily, such as should be saved."
It was later glossators who substituted, for the vague
phrase "this thing," the words "the Church."

Again and again St. Paul and St. John re-echo
this word "The Fellowship." St. Paul calls it the
Christian "mystery" : it was something that

transcended sex, transcended social and intellectual distinctions, transcended race and nationality, making all men sharers in the same Mystical Body, the "one new man." On its inward side, it was Christ within, the hope of glory. It was an atmosphere of reconciling peace. Over and over he pleads for the maintenance of this coherence, this "unity of the Spirit in the bond of peace." He sought to make the separate congregations he had founded, stretch out hands to one another across time and distance, not in any external oneness of ecclesiastical polity, but in this Fellowship. For to deny or repudiate the Fellowship is to be an offence unto the Spirit. The sin of sins which hinders the manifestation of the Spirit in the world—and this is true in our day as in the beginning—is the offence against spiritual unity, Fellowship.

But how, according to the New Testament, did this new creation manifest itself to the world ? At first men were struck by the element of sheer marvel, the ecstasies, the glossalalia, the contagion that lifted men on to a new plane of Spirit-life, and gave them command and direction of powers of healing, of utterance, of revitalisation. But it is not these things which give us the differentia by which we estimate the event of Pentecost. The highest of all the new gifts of life which flowed into, or were evoked within, the hearts of men at Pentecost was, as St. Paul tells us, in a passage which is the holiest flower of New Testament inspiration, Love, accompanied by Faith and Hope. These are the things that abide, when prophecies, healings, visions, insights, pass away. Temporary or sporadic manifestations may vary in spiritual outpourings; but this is constant and abiding—the moral touchstone of every spiritual movement—Love : Love leaning on Faith in a great deed of love—Love resting on a Divine Promise, and looking forward with Hope and expectancy shining in her eyes. The *moral* efficiency of the Fellowship lies in its fruits, of which Love is the first. And the method or law by which this new society operates in the world, is Love's method— sacrifice. The early Fellowship expressed itself in its central rite by the symbol of the " one loaf," an inexhaustible Loaf to be broken, a living sacrifice for the need of a hungry world. This was the inner essence of all true worship—adoration of the " Broken Body " issuing in dedication to sacrificial service.

But all this resulted from its *religious* efficacy, which lay in its corporate intuition of Divine Truth. It is in the sharing of vision that the unity of the Fellowship is consummated. " That which we have seen and heard declare we unto you that you may have fellowship with us. And the Fellowship— ours—is with the Father and with His Son Jesus Christ." Moreover it is " together *with all the saints* " that the believer comes to " comprehend what is the length and breadth and depth and height, and to know the love of Christ which passeth knowledge." Vision is not, of course, denied to the solitary seeker. "When thou prayest, enter into thy closet," said Jesus. But He said also, "Where two or three are gathered together in My name, there am I in the midst to bless." For the vision is best realised in the fellowship of the two or three, not in the great assembly. Into the mass-meeting men come to declare truth; but into the group, to seek it. And it is in the little group that the inward and spiritual communion "with all the saints" is best realised, not in mass contacts or imposing outward organisation. "God is the place where spirits blend," not necessarily where masses gather. It is in the intermingling of soul with soul in holy yearning that the light breaks, and vision comes. Would God we could recover this way of loyalty to the Fellowship to-day, that our vision might be renewed, and our life revived!

VIII. THE MIND OF THE FELLOWSHIP

And here we approach the central point in our enquiry into the New Testament experience. What was the nature of the spiritual vision won in the Fellowship? There were two main factors in the vision; and the phrase we lately quoted from St. Paul—"the love of Christ"—gives us the clue to them both. We can only state them in the briefest outline. (a) The first was *an insight into the meaning of the Cross.* For though the Fellowship was "in the Spirit," the early Christians never did describe the central thing in their experience as belief in the presence and power of the Holy Spirit. As Principal Denney has pointed out, there is no such expression in the New Testament as believing in the Holy Ghost. The Spirit is the experience itself—an experience which comes through faith in the crucified Jesus. The New Testament experience was first and foremost an intuitive vision, an "assurance that God is sin-bearing Love." . . . "To have that assurance" (we quote again from Principal Denney), "in overwhelming strength—as the Apostle had it through faith in Christ—is to be full of the Holy Spirit." In other words, the Fellowship achieved the ecstatic insight, born of penitence, that God Himself was actively operating in them, through Jesus, to disclose the central reality of the Divine Life as a Forgiving Heart of Love, and to impart His forgiveness.

(b) The second main element in the New Testament experience is the inevitable consequence of this. If the Cross, where we see God as sin-bearing Love, is central in the experience, then the crucified and risen *Jesus is Lord*. Amid the multitude of voices professing to be the work of the Spirit, there was, for the leaders of the early Church, but one infallible religious test. Only the Spirit that led men to the confession : "Jesus is Lord," could be the genuine Spirit of God. Paul had doubtless in view those cults, of which the mystery-religions were examples, where the initiates confessed this, that, and the other revealer as Lord. The test was a test of history. " The historic Jesus is the Master of all Life, the Lord of Glory." St. John slightly alters the statement, to combat the Gnostic heresies which " divided Christ," and spoke of a " Christ-spirit " (or æon) distinct from Jesus : " Every Spirit that confesses Jesus as Christ come in the flesh is of God, and every spirit that confesses not Jesus as Christ come in the flesh is not of God." It is the earliest, shortest, and perhaps the most efficient of all the creeds : " Jesus is Lord." " Thou art the Christ," said Peter at Cæsarea Philippi. And on the streets of Jerusalem at Pentecost he said, " God has made both Lord and Christ this very Jesus whom you crucified."

IX. THE MEANING OF THE SPIRIT

What, then, was this Divine Spirit, which, when it broke into utterance in a human heart, declared in adoration, " Jesus is Lord " ? The startling truth is that St. Paul hardly distinguishes between the Spirit and God and Christ at all. " You," he says to the Romans, " are not in the flesh but in *the Spirit*, since *the Spirit of God* dwells in you. Anyone who does not possess *the Spirit of Christ* does not belong to Him." (Rom. viii. 9-11.) There, in almost the same dip of the pen, he uses the terms, " Spirit," " Spirit of God," " Spirit of Christ " as clearly interchangeable. Nor is it otherwise where he says : " Now there are varieties of gifts but the same *Spirit*, varieties of service but the same *Lord*, varieties of workings but the same *God* who works all things in all." (1 Cor. xii. 4-6.) When we think of gifts we think of the bestower as Spirit ; when we think of services we think of Jesus " the Servant " as Lord of service ; when we think of the energies which gifts and services alike imply we think of God, whose energy it is that works through all. Nor otherwise must we read the word : " There is one Body, and one *Spirit* . . . one hope . . . one *Lord*, one faith, one baptism, one *God and Father* of all, who is over all, and through all, and in all." (Eph. iv. 4-6.) Spirit, Lord, and God the Father, all are one in the one immanent Divine Spirit that pervades nature, humanity, and Fellowship alike. The language of these remarkable documents —" the most free-thinking book in the world "— is pre-eminently the language of experience, the utterance of thought that is plastic, and flows into endless forms. For the Spirit that confesses Jesus is the same Spirit that confesses God the Father too. " God hath sent forth *the Spirit*." Yes, but what Spirit ? " God hath sent forth the Spirit of *His Son*, into your hearts." To what end ? " Crying, ' Abba, *Father*.' " (Gal. iv. 6.) Do we hesitate a moment about identifying " the Holy Spirit " with " the Spirit of His Son," " the Spirit of Christ " ? Then let us listen yet again to St. Paul: " Now the Lord *is* the Spirit!" (2 Cor. iii. 17)

All this is the language of experience which is touching the very heart and centre of Reality, and realising its spiritual oneness. It is not the language of the merely theological mind, which is so fond of making abstract distinctions and elevating them into self-existent entities. There is just one profound suggestion in St. Paul's letters as to the ultimate rationale of the Divine Spirit. "What human being," he says, "can know the thoughts of a man save the man's own inner spirit? So, too, no one knows the thoughts of God except the Spirit of God." (1 Cor. ii. 10f.) In short, Paul here suggests that the Spirit is what we in modern terms would call the Self-consciousness of God. And in the same significant passage he describes this Divine Self-consciousness as exploring the deeps of God's vast mind. All things, including the mind of man, are within this mighty ocean of Spirit-life; so that the Divine Self-consciousness is present in the human spirit—man's self-consciousness. It explores man's mind and conscience, as the ocean-tide invades the creek; or as the holy, revealing sunlight steals into the dark caves of earth. It searches out all the recesses of man's spirit with tireless, beneficent intent, even as the sunlight in those dark places of the earth, awakening all that is living there to a new effort after life—holiness. And even as it searches, it identifies itself, in the unsullied tenderness which is only possible to perfect Purity, with all man's brokenness, failures, shames, bearing back a message of pleading on his behalf to the throne of God's heart. For elsewhere the Apostle says, " He who searches the human heart knows what is in the mind of the Spirit, since the Spirit pleads before God for His people." (Rom. viii. 27.) He who is the Advocate with men for God, is also the Advocate for men before God's throne. Nor is there any contradiction in the New Testament experience, when St. John tells us our Advocate with the Father is " Jesus Christ the Righteous," or when the writer of the Epistle to the Hebrews tells us that it is He who, " touched with the feeling of our infirmities," yet " saintly, innocent, unstained, lifted high above the heavens," has become our eternal " High Priest," and now " appears in the presence of God on our behalf."

But—to return for a moment to this wonderful passage in St. Paul about the Self-consciousness of God—this all-inclusive, immanent, Divine Spirit is God actively willing to disclose His mind to man. Like the revealing sunlight it unveils the deepest treasures of God's heart to the human heart. Where then, and how, does the heart of man learn these mysteries of Godhead ? How does the Spirit unveil them ? Once more, in the end of that wonderful second chapter of 1st Cor., Paul answers in a word confirming all that has been said : "We have the mind of Christ." (1 Cor. ii. 16.) The mind of Christ ! The Christian's apprehension of God can no longer be separated from Christ. It includes, but far transcends, all that he has ever known of God

in other ways. It is an overwhelming vision, this—
that the great unseen Power, operating from the
central deeps of the Universe, must in His essential
nature be what Christ was. It is the impression of
a peerless Personality, awakening feelings of awe,
reverence, humility—the reverence which only the
vision of majestic Meekness, infinite Humility can
awaken. God is Humility, the humblest Slave in
His universe. It was the constraint of Will evoked
by a soul of flawless purity—the constraint which
only an urgent, tireless, ever-active Holiness that
yearns and hopes for the world, on and ever on, can
evoke. God is Holiness, the pure Will that longs
and labours to purify. It was the impact of an
overwhelming deed in human history awakening
redemption-gratitude, love,—the love which only
uttermost Love can awaken. God is Love—the
tender Heart that agonises to redeem. It was the
uplifting and expanding of the heart awakened by
the sympathy of Christ—an uplift which only an
exhaustless capacity for fellowship can awaken.
And such is God who made us for Himself. That is
the end of His creative activity—a Fellowship of all
souls in Him. In a very real sense, God is Fellowship. And the vision makes us restless, until in the
Fellowship of all the faithful we find at length our
true rest in Him.

And all this vision of God through Christ we
receive in the Holy Spirit, the Spirit of the indwelling
God, which is for the Christian the Spirit of the living,

ever-present Christ. This is the New Testament Experience.

And see now how this vision expands. Even Paul makes us see this energy of the immanent, Divine Will spread out through the whole of life and all creation's bounds—God's Holy Purpose driven forward by an unswerving, infinite Desire. The whole creation is groaning and struggling together until now, under the impulse of this redeeming grace, this self-effacing, self-sacrificing Spirit of God. Every renewing of the face of Nature in springtime—every fresh blade of grass, every green leaf on the tree, every new beginning in the birth of living things, as well as every saint agonising and every prodigal returning— is crying, "Holy, holy, holy is the Lord," and the cry is not only a prayer but a prophecy—a prophecy of the final victory of the Cross, and of the Holy Fellowship of all true souls in God.

The Spirit is the Christian Hertha, the Christian Brahma—if we may say so, reverently, without being misunderstood : the Spirit which unfolds in Nature and the Spirit which broods above Nature to draw out that unfolding ; the Spirit which struggles upward in man as religious aspiration—seeking the Fellowship Divine, and the Spirit above the aspiring soul, kindling flashes of vision into the truth of things ; the Spirit of the Divine Son who knows and confesses the Father, and the Spirit of the Father, imparting Himself wholly to the Son " in whom He is well-pleased " ; the Spirit in the penitent who breathes his sorrowful confession, and the Spirit that flows into the penitent with quickening and renewing power ; the Spirit in the believer, which confesses the Lordship of the crucified and risen Jesus, and the Spirit of the glorified Christ, incarnating Himself in the Mystical Body, the believing Fellowship ; that in us which prays, the Burden of the prayer, the Hearer and the Answerer as well. " The Search, and the sought, and the seeker : the soul and the body that is."

For behold I am with you, and in you, and of you : look forth now
and see. . . .
I am in thee to save thee
As my soul in thee saith ;
Give thou as I gave thee,
Thy life-blood and breath.
Green leaves of thy labour, white flowers of thy thought, and red
fruit of thy death.

Or again, in simpler words, which may be some atonement, if the lines thus appropriated are felt to be too pagan :

His that gentle voice we hear,
Soft as the breath of even,
That checks each fault, and calms each fear
And speaks of heaven.
And every virtue we possess,
And every victory won,
And every thought of holiness,
Are His alone.

X. THE TEST OF THE EXPERIENCE

Is this New Testament experience a mere subjective hallucination ? Apply the one test that satisfies, the test of moral values. Have all the great moral and spiritual achievements, the reforms, the revivals, the regenerations, the heroisms, the martyrdoms, confessedly accomplished by the help of this Divine Spirit that leads us into Truth, been the result of illusion ? Can God's universe be built so as to win its ends by fraud and self-deception ? To say so is the ultimate blasphemy. So Jesus said, in His passionate vindication of the presence of the Spirit of God in Himself. " Whosoever speaketh a word against the Son of Man, it shall be forgiven him, but he that shall blaspheme against the Holy Ghost it shall not be forgiven him, neither in this world, neither in the world to come." Sin as you will— He seems to say—as mere men groping blindly in the dark, and you are still within the reach of forgiveness, for it is not the action of your enlightened self. But sin against the blazing light of the Spirit's presence, deny and mock Its power, call the white and holy deeds It works among men deeds of darkness, and you cannot be forgiven : you have sunk into the eternal blindness from which even the light of God's Spirit cannot awaken you ; you have diabolised yourself, and can only be cast out.

XI. OUR RECOVERY OF THE NEW TESTAMENT EXPERIENCE

What is the supreme need of the Church to-day ? Is it not that she may reach back once again into the light and warmth of this New Testament Experience ?

Who was Jesus of Nazareth?

The vision has faded. False conceptions have crept into the mind of the Church. The flood-gates are all but closed against the Spirit. What, then, are the essentials necessary to the recovery of life and power and vision ?

(1) The first is an utter and wholehearted surrender of the Church to the *faith that the living Lord is present in her midst*, here and now ; that she lives because He lives—and for no other reason ; and that He will be with her alway even unto the end of the world.

(2) The second, we are persuaded, is *freedom*. The true pilgrim Church cannot journey in fetters or in cerements. " But," someone may interject, " truth is not won by the spirit that despises the past : reverence is the first essential—reverence for the ancient tradition." Yes, reverence for the past, by all means. But reverence is not slavery, not spiritual thraldom. Reverence is not the binding of oneself to the dead letter : it is emulating the spirit that fought, amid dimmer lights, the battle of faith. The Church must give up the pathetic obsession that what was the utterance of the living faith of a long past must continue to be the expression of this living, growing thing forever. It is her own loyalty, her present witness to her Lord the Church is ever called on to declare. And liberty is the only air which loyalty can breathe. Freedom, not bondage to ancient formulæ, is the second essential.

(3) And the third is a firmer grasp of *the conviction*

that the Holy Spirit, the Spirit of the Risen Christ, *is waiting to lead us into all the Truth*—into all the unsearchable riches of the Reality whose throbbing heart-beat was felt by the company of the Upper Room. God has yet much light to break out of His Word. There must be a complete abandonment of the faithless misgiving, the fear, that this may lead us out of Christ into something strangely, coldly different. The Church is to grow up into Christ in all things. He is " *the* Truth "; there can be no " Truth " which leads out of Him.

(4) And the fourth essential is *sincerity*, singleness of heart. For all roads built by sincerity lead finally to God. Blessed are the single-hearted, for they alone shall see Christ. And it was for vision— for *this* vision—the Church was primarily created. It is not new prophets, still less little Christs, the Church must look for, but true witnesses to Christ, eye-witnesses, men and women who have *seen* the Lord.

(5) And the last and not the least of these essentials is *a recovery of the sense of the Fellowship :* a fresh baptism of Love—the love that binds the loyal to their crucified Redeemer, making all one in Him. Our Christian memories, yea, and our Christian hopes of the Kingdom, can only be made alive by love, love in the Fellowship which transcends past, present, and future, when it rises to the mountain-top of holy vision, whence it surveys in a single unity of insight all that we cannot make

present to our momentary view, or catch in our fleeting emotion.

Yes, the true Church of Christ is pre-eminently the Community that sees, the Fellowship that enjoys a present experience, rather than the Community that remembers. The Fellowship is the organism created to receive that experience ; not an organisation for conserving tradition. And when we are confronted by one last challenge of this view, when we are told that the great rite enshrined in the heart of the Church is a sacrament of remembrance, we answer by asking, In what sense is it such ? Is it an act of sitting still in passive contemplation of one far-off Divine event from which the whole creation is swiftly receding ? Nay, not such remembering is our sacrament. We die into Christ's death, and rise again into His risen life, in which all the Fellowship participates. We do, indeed, remember Christ after the flesh : we dare not drag the roots of our Christian experience out of history. Every honest attempt to see Him as He was is to be welcomed ; but only so that we may learn more of His eternal significance. For the Christ with whom we hold personal and present fellowship is Christ as He is, the Christ after the Spirit, the Christ who labours and strives in the hearts of the loyal for the coming of His kingdom among men.

And the Divine vocation of the Fellowship on earth is the ever renewed confession of this living Jesus as Lord. The Church is called on to confess, and again confess, no matter what the obstacles in the way may be. When she ceases to do so, she is no longer fulfilling her function on the earth. She must recapture the New Testament Experience, make it her own, and utter it forth in words that sincerely mean what they say. It may not be amiss, therefore, to end these studies with the following brief and simple confession of the Faith:

I BELIEVE IN GOD, THROUGH JESUS CHRIST, HIS ONLY SON, OUR LORD:

> because I acknowledge and hallow in my heart Christ's unshareable partnership with God; and in Him behold the Father, to whom all worlds belong.

I GIVE MYSELF TO GOD, WHO WAS IN CHRIST RECONCILING THE WORLD TO HIMSELF:

> because I recognise that Christ's Divine Vocation was to be God's Forgiveness among men; and that His Passion was the Agony of the sin-bearing God.

I SHARE THE ASSURANCE THAT THE LIVING CHRIST IS PRESENT NOW AND ALWAYS IN THE FELLOWSHIP OF THE FAITHFUL, LABOURING FOR THE COMING OF HIS KINGDOM AMONG MEN:

> because I accept the Spirit's testimony that Jesus is alive and unholden of death; and that He is still awakening the souls of men to Eternal Truth and Eternal Life.

Who was Jesus of Nazareth?

AND FINALLY I AM PERSUADED THAT ALL THE REDEEMED SHALL LIVE FOREVER WITH HIM AND REIGN WITH HIM IN A PERFECTED AND UNSHAKABLE KINGDOM :

because He that hath promised is faithful;
to Him be the glory, forever and ever. Amen.

Headley Brothers, 18, Devonshire Street, E.C.2; and Ashford, Kent.

Trieste

Trieste Publishing has a massive catalogue of classic book titles. Our aim is to provide readers with the highest quality reproductions of fiction and non-fiction literature that has stood the test of time. The many thousands of books in our collection have been sourced from libraries and private collections around the world.

The titles that Trieste Publishing has chosen to be part of the collection have been scanned to simulate the original. Our readers see the books the same way that their first readers did decades or a hundred or more years ago. Books from that period are often spoiled by imperfections that did not exist in the original. Imperfections could be in the form of blurred text, photographs, or missing pages. It is highly unlikely that this would occur with one of our books. Our extensive quality control ensures that the readers of Trieste Publishing's books will be delighted with their purchase. Our staff has thoroughly reviewed every page of all the books in the collection, repairing, or if necessary, rejecting titles that are not of the highest quality. This process ensures that the reader of one of Trieste Publishing's titles receives a volume that faithfully reproduces the original, and to the maximum degree possible, gives them the experience of owning the original work.

We pride ourselves on not only creating a pathway to an extensive reservoir of books of the finest quality, but also providing value to every one of our readers. Generally, Trieste books are purchased singly - on demand, however they may also be purchased in bulk. Readers interested in bulk purchases are invited to contact us directly to enquire about our tailored bulk rates. Email: customerservice@triestepublishing.com

You May Also Like

The Letters of a Woman who Was, by the Woman

Helen Field Robertson

ISBN: 9780649630837
Paperback: 132 pages
Dimensions: 6.14 x 0.28 x 9.21 inches
Language: eng

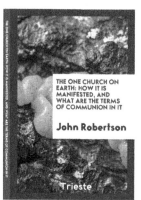

The One Church on Earth: How It Is Manifested, and What Are the Terms of Communion in It

John Robertson

ISBN: 9780649661916
Paperback: 168 pages
Dimensions: 6.14 x 0.36 x 9.21 inches
Language: eng

www.triestepublishing.com

You May Also Like

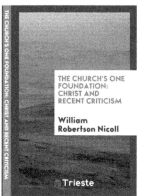

ISBN: 9780649549672
Paperback: 248 pages
Dimensions: 6.14 x 0.52 x 9.21 inches
Language: eng

The Church's One Foundation: Christ and Recent Criticism

William Robertson Nicoll

ISBN: 9780649660339
Paperback: 174 pages
Dimensions: 5.5 x 0.37 x 8.5 inches
Language: eng

Ochil Idylls and Other Poems

James Logie Robertson (Hugh Haliburton)

You May Also Like

ISBN: 9780649333158
Paperback: 84 pages
Dimensions: 6.14 x 0.17 x 9.21 inches
Language: eng

Report of the Department of Farms and Markets, pp. 5-71

Various

ISBN: 9780649324132
Paperback: 78 pages
Dimensions: 6.14 x 0.16 x 9.21 inches
Language: eng

Catalogue of the Episcopal Theological School in Cambridge Massachusetts, 1891-1892

Various

www.triestepublishing.com

You May Also Like

Three Hundred Tested Recipes

Various

ISBN: 9780649352142
Paperback: 88 pages
Dimensions: 6.14 x 0.18 x 9.21 inches
Language: eng

A Basket of Fragments

Anonymous

ISBN: 9780649419418
Paperback: 108 pages
Dimensions: 6.14 x 0.22 x 9.21 inches
Language: eng

Find more of our titles on our website. We have a selection of thousands of titles that will interest you. Please visit

www.triestepublishing.com